All about home baking

Behold the proud beauty of it.
Imagine its fresh-baked fragrance, its melting taste.
This book is dedicated to just such excellent baking

Such baking casts a magic spell

ALL
ABOUT
HOME BAKING

CONSUMER SERVICE DEPARTMENT
GENERAL FOODS CORPORATION · NEW YORK

Contents of
All About Home Baking

✿

The stage all set to make a butter cake

It's a Wise Woman
Who Knows Her Baking Rules

☼

HAVE you ever wished you were blessed with "a born knack for baking"? Stop your wishing! There's no such thing to be had! Baking skill is made and not born. It takes no special gift, no magic touch, to work wonders with a mixing bowl. Some old-fashioned cooks, true enough, seemingly tossed things together and achieved glorious results. But the secret there was long practice. Doing a job over and over again does give one a sense of how things should look and feel; it builds up judgment which may take the place of rules.

Today's busy women, however, will not take time to learn their tricks that way, and modern knowledge makes it unnecessary. The progressive homemaker walks right up to Science and says "You tell me how." It's this love of right method, this desire to do things with a reason—in *proved* ways, that has simplified home baking and made its results more certain.

Here, in this book, there are tested ways to perfect baking. Whether you're a beginner or an old hand at the game, the things you learn here will make your baking better, easier, and more fun!

The recipes given are the result of months of experiments and careful development. They have all been tested and retested, checked and rechecked in the General Foods Kitchens. They are dependable in every way. Make these recipes your very own. Use them confidently. They'll make your baking one triumph after another.

This book also introduces a new simplified method of perfecting your mixing technic—*the key step method.* As you read these pages, you will discover that many baked things are related. They branch from a few basic recipes. Each basic recipe is distinguished by certain characteristic key steps in the mixing process. To master all baking —master these key steps. The picture method makes it easy.

Because the modern hostess serves charmingly, too, All About Home Baking includes some clever new ideas for parties and everyday occasions all through the year. Lovely table settings. Novel decorations. New menu surprises. For buffet suppers . . . luncheons . . . teas . . . all sorts of festive affairs.

Now let's begin our baking adventure! Let's start with the basic rules and follow each one carefully.

1. *Be orderly*

    Do your planning before you start. Choose your recipe, read it through carefully, understand it clearly. Collect all the ingredients it calls for in their order; assemble all the utensils you will need on your work table. Cultivate the do-it-right habit. It makes the job a joy, and it saves you time, money, and many a worried moment in your baking.

2. *Use good tools*

    Good tools simplify baking. They enable you to do things more easily, more accurately. They speed up mixing and help you to achieve uniformly successful results. Check up your utensils with the illustration opposite. Here are: standard measuring cup and spoons, a wooden mixing paddle, slotted spoon, scoop, rubber scraper, steel spatula, cutting knives, rotary egg beater, wire whisk, flour sieve, small sieve, mixing bowls with rounded bottoms, baking pans, pastry brush, pastry blender, biscuit cutter, wire cake tester, wire cake rack, oven thermometer, candy thermometer, pair of scissors, and a cake decorator with assorted tips.

3. *Choose good ingredients*

    You can't do first-rate baking with second-rate materials. Be sure your ingredients are strictly fresh and of the finest quality. A whole chapter of this book is devoted to explaining the type of baking powder, the kind of flour, and other baking ingredients to use for finest results. Read it. Clear up once and for all those baking troubles which result from inferior or inappropriate materials. (See pages 10 to 15.)

Use good tools to insure baking success

4. *Measure accurately*

   That's a baking *"must."* The best materials in the world—the greatest skill in mixing—cannot overcome mistakes in the amounts of ingredients. To assure uniformly successful results, the recipes in this book are developed with a definite measuring technic. All measurements are level. The methods for measuring adopted by cooking authorities are fully described in one of the following chapters. Before you put your hand to a mixing spoon again, be sure to read it. It will give you a new confidence in all your baking, and make it easier than ever before. (See pages 16 to 22.)

5. *Mix carefully*

   There are several basic methods of performing the mixing job for each type of baking. These methods are clearly described and illustrated, step by step, in the recipe sections of this book. Study them, follow them carefully. There's a real thrill in learning to do things with a reason.

6. *Know your pans and oven, and how to cool your cakes*

   The actual baking process is exceedingly important. Proper pans and the best way to use them, correct oven temperatures, time-tables for baking, correct cooling of cakes after baking—all are fully discussed in a chapter on these last but not least steps toward successful baking. (See pages 23 to 28.)

Ingredients—
The Inside Story of Baking Success

✲

T O bake good things—put good things into them! There's the
start of the story. You can't get light, tender textures and delicate flavors with inferior ingredients.

That's no news, you say? You wouldn't dream of using anything
but fresh, high-grade ingredients? Good! But there's more to the
story than that. This is a subject worth a little study.

Quality isn't the only way in which ingredients vary. There's a
difference in *kinds*. Baking powders behave differently and all cannot be used in the same amounts. All flours are not alike. They're
not all suited to every need.

Suppose, for instance, that a recipe calls for two level teaspoons
of baking powder. Will two teaspoons of *any* baking powder do?
Suppose the recipe calls for cake flour. Will you get as perfect a cake
if you use ordinary flour instead?

Of course not! And the reason is simple. All good recipes are
carefully worked out and tested with certain definite products. The
nature of these products—the job they do—decides the kind and
proportion called for in the recipe. If you substitute ingredients
which behave differently you change the recipe. The results may be
quite disappointing.

The rest of this chapter will open your eyes to some important
differences in baking ingredients. It will tell you why the *kind* of
flour and the *kind* of baking powder used in developing the recipes
in this book give such excellent results. It will show you why it's
important to match these recipes in every way—ingredient for ingredient, measurement for measurement—if you want them to bring
you in your kitchen the same tiptop results they bring in the General Foods Kitchens every time they are used.

Baking Powder—The Star Performer

Baking powder is a small part of any given recipe—yet it plays
such an important rôle that it can make a great difference in the success you get in baking.

Baking powders cause doughs and batters to "rise." There is
nothing mysterious about this. There are certain chemical substances in baking powders. When moisture and heat are applied,
these chemicals react to form carbon-dioxide gas. As this gas rises,
it stretches the dough or batter and makes it light or porous and
holds it that way until the oven has done its work. This is known as

Best baking calls for quality ingredients with recipes developed for the products used. Cinnamon rolls like these tell of such a partnership

Good materials and good recipes

the leavening process and must be an even, controlled action.

All baking powders are required by law to be made of pure, wholesome ingredients. And they *all* give off leavening gas. But— they vary in the speed of their reaction and in the quantity of their gas lost from the surface of batters during mixing. That is why different types of baking powders require different amounts to do a job. A recipe developed with one baking powder should not be used with another without readjusting the amount used, unless the same amount is recommended for both.

So red-letter this on your list of baking rules: To get perfect leavening—the kind of leavening that will give you the fine, light texture, the velvety crumb, and the even shape of a tiptop cake— be sure that you use the baking powder which is called for in your recipe; and be sure that you use the exact amount called for.

Perfect Leavening and Maximum Protection

In the recipes in this book, Calumet Baking Powder is used. Calumet Baking Powder has a *double* leavening action, the result of a *combination* of two gas-releasing ingredients. For this reason, Calumet is known as "the Double-Acting Baking Powder," and is of the combination type.

Calumet's two leavening actions are perfectly controlled and timed to give a maximum protection in baking. This is how they work.

As soon as you add liquid to dry ingredients, Calumet's first action begins. Right before your eyes, hundreds of tiny bubbles are rising through the batter. This gets the leavening off to a good start.

BUT—only part of the gas is released in the mixing bowl. Calumet's second action waits. In the heat of the oven, this second action gets to work. Steadily, evenly, hundreds of new tiny bubbles swell through the batter and continue the leavening. Up! . . . up! . . . they keep raising the batter and hold it high and light. Thanks to these two actions, Calumet protects your baking from start to finish.

Follow Calumet's Economical Proportion

Due to the perfect timing and efficiency of its double leavening action, the Calumet proportion is very economical. General directions are printed on the label of the Calumet can: "Use 1 level teaspoon of Calumet Baking Powder for each cup of sifted flour." This amount is only one-half to two-thirds the amount recommended by many other manufacturers.

Most of the recipes in this book call for this proportion. In some recipes, however, the number of eggs, the type of flour, or the nature of other ingredients makes slightly more or less advisable. But every recipe calling for baking powder has been tested again and again

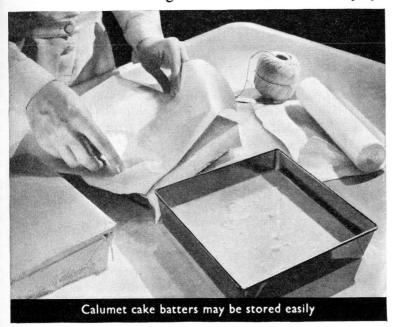

Calumet cake batters may be stored easily

and has been carefully built with exactly the right proportions to give you the full advantage of Calumet's balanced Double-Action.

Now!—Cake Batters Can Wait!

We explained on page 12 how Calumet's second action gets under way when the batter goes in the oven. Think what it means!

Calumet batters can be stored until you are ready to bake them.

For instance, you can mix up a batch of batter—enough for three different cakes. You can divide this batter into three pans, you can store them away, and pop them into the oven as you need them—on three different days. Three glorious desserts from one mixing job! And the cake that waits longest will be as perfect as the one that is baked first. The picture above will show you how it's done.

Try this new baking idea. It saves time. It saves work. Just use the basic recipe given on page 138 for Miracle Cake.

Flour—There are Different Kinds for Home Baking

Now don't say—"Oh, yes, I know there are dozens of different brands of flour." For we don't mean *brands*—we mean *kinds*. And to get really successful results, you must choose the kind of flour best suited to the kind of thing you are baking.

Bread, for instance, requires a flour milled from *hard* or *strong* wheat which contains a tenacious, elastic gluten. This strong gluten is excellent for the slow leavening action of yeast used in bread dough. But for cakes, tender quick breads, and pastries, a very different kind of flour is needed—one of fine, pliable gluten quality which yields readily to the action of baking powder and other quick leaveners, and gives a delicate structure to baked products. Such a flour is Swans Down Cake Flour. It is specially milled from *soft* winter wheat; it contains only a small amount of gluten and that gluten is delicate and tender. Swans Down gives a lightness and tenderness to fine baking that you cannot expect from ordinary flour.

The Swans Down Way to Quality

In this book, Swans Down Cake Flour is specified for all of the cakes and many quick breads. Swans Down, you know, is the *original* cake flour—and you might almost call it the "blue ribbon flour." For at state and county fairs, more prize-winning cakes are made with Swans Down than with any other one cake flour.

Cakes made with Swans Down have a silky-smooth texture and a marvelous delicacy. It gives all your quality baking—cakes, pastries, waffles, shortcakes, quick-bread specialties—a fineness and tenderness that simply cannot be matched by ordinary flour.

Swans Down gluten is, of course, the secret. Swans Down is made from select winter wheat—and only the choicest part of the wheat kernel is used. It takes 100 pounds of soft, winter wheat to make 26 pounds of Swans Down Cake Flour.

Swans Down is also specially milled. It is ground and reground, sifted and resifted through fine silken sieves until it is *27 times as fine as ordinary flour*. The careful milling which Swans Down Cake Flour undergoes is so closely controlled at every step that the final quality of the flour never varies.

You'll find the Swans Down way thriftier, too. Even the simplest economy cakes are wonderfully tender and light when made with Swans Down. To begin to approximate as fine a cake with ordinary flour, you'd have to use more eggs and more shortening.

Keep your flour in a dry, cool, well-aired place. If you suspect that your flour has become damp, sift it five or six times before the opened door of a heated oven; then cool it before using.

Sugar, Shortening, Liquids, and Eggs

Confectioners' sugar is the finest white sugar made. It is used principally for frostings. Powdered sugar comes next. Then granulated sugar, which comes in different grades. Unless some other kind is called for, always use fine granulated sugar. Coarse sugar makes a coarse texture. Brown sugar and maple sugar add flavor to baked things in addition to sweetening them.

Shortening makes doughs and batters "short" or tender. The shortening power of different substances varies according to the per cent of fat contained, but, in most recipes, shortenings may be used interchangeably. Butter is especially good in cakes; a combination using half butter is often preferred in pie crust and shortcakes. When unsalted fat is substituted for butter, salt must be added to the recipe for flavor. Whatever the shortening you use, be sure that it is fresh and sweet; for the flavor of shortening that is rancid can always be detected in finished baking.

Sweet or sour milk and cream, buttermilk, water, or fruit juices may be used in baking. Sweet milk should be used when recipes call for milk. In using sour milk or cream, it is best to use quickly soured products, as they have better flavor than those soured slowly. Dry, powdered, evaporated, and condensed milk may also be used.

Use eggs of fine quality. They may be fresh-gathered or cold storage. When eggs are to be beaten, remove them from refrigerator several hours before using as they beat lighter and more quickly when not too cold. This is most important in making angel food or sponge cakes which depend solely on eggs for leavening.

Chocolate, Coconut, and Flavorings

Chocolate is a favorite flavor in many baked products. *Baker's Unsweetened Chocolate* is specified in the recipes in this book. Its rich natural flavor and smooth texture make it a universal choice. The half-pound cake of Baker's Unsweetened Chocolate is grooved deeply in eight squares of one ounce each. These deep markings enable you to break off a square evenly and easily.

Coconut is friendly to all home baking. Its snowy shreds bring flavor and decoration to cakes, pies, cookies, and a host of good desserts. *Baker's Coconut, Southern Style,* is fresh-grated coconut, slightly sweetened and packed, without coconut milk, in air-tight cans. Its long, lacy shred is especially appropriate for sprinkling over frosted cakes, pies, tarts. For ease in measuring, use it from the can in the amounts given in the recipes. *Baker's Coconut, Premium Shred,* is finely shredded and sugar-cured. It is carefully packaged in moisture-proof cartons that are triple-sealed to insure freshness.

Of all flavorings vanilla is perhaps the most popular. Lemon, orange, and almond are also great favorites. Many delicate, delicious blends may be produced by skillfully combining different flavors. Lemon and vanilla, or rose and almond give a subtle flavor.

Spices must be fresh and of good quality. Measure them very carefully and do not be too lavish with them, for too much spice disguises the delicate flavor of cake. Spices should be sifted with the flour to mix them well with other ingredients.

Measuring—there's a right and wrong way

Measuring—
How To Play Fair With Recipes

☼

WHEN her cake failed, or her biscuits turned out sadly, the old-fashioned housewife sighed and said, "Bad luck!" However, the chances are that it wasn't her luck that was wrong; it was her measuring. In those days, you see, recipes were handed down from mother to daughter, with such measurements as "enough flour to make a nice stiffness" . . . "butter the size of an egg" . . . "a generous goblet of sugar" . . . "as much saleratus as will lie on a penny." And when daughter's cake couldn't quite hold a candle to mother's, it very likely was because her idea of "a nice stiffness," or "the size of an egg" was different from mother's.

For exactly how much is "enough flour to make a nice stiffness"? Is the butter to be the size of a small egg or a large egg? How measure a generous goblet of sugar?

Today, it's a happier story. Recipes travel all over the land; and thanks to the efforts of food experts, they all talk one language. A language that enables *every* woman to achieve correct measurements *every* time—standard measurements.

Always use standard measurements. Standard measuring equipment for cooking consists of a standard cup and a set of standard

16

measuring spoons. (See illustration on page 9.) You can buy them in almost any town. But wherever you buy them, be sure they conform to the specifications adopted by the United States Bureau of Standards. These are as follows:

A standard measuring cup is an accurate half-pint measure—the equivalent of 16 level tablespoons. It is grooved on one side to read ¼, ½, and ¾; on the other, to read ⅓ and ⅔.

Standard measuring spoons include one tablespoon, one teaspoon, one-half teaspoon, and one-quarter teaspoon. The tablespoon is the equivalent of 3 teaspoons.

The difference between standard measurements and hit-or-miss measurements may be understood from the illustration on page 16. Here "butter the size of an egg," any kitchen cup of milk, and a "heaping" cup of flour are amounts that are ever variable, while the standard level measuring tablespoon of butter, the standard measuring cup of milk, and the standard measuring cup of sifted flour, would be the same time and again, and uniform in every kitchen.

Acceptable recipes today are developed with this standard measuring equipment. It is always used in the General Foods Kitchens. Play fair with these measurements—and they'll play fair with you.

Always use level measurements. All measurements are level. That's the success rule of every truly modern recipe.

Level measuring is so important, in fact, that a definite technic has been worked out for making the measurements of the various ingredients level. These technics have been so standardized that the amounts obtained are very uniform. You'll find this information carefully described and illustrated on pages 16 to 20.

All the recipes in this book have been developed in the General Foods Kitchens, with standard level measurements. Every recipe has been made up time and again. Each ingredient and measurement has been carefully checked and rechecked. Each mixing technic has been carefully perfected. The methods given here are simple and practical. They are used by experts the country over; yet even a new bride can use them easily and successfully.

Flour—Only One Accurate Way to Measure It

Flour is one of the easiest of all ingredients to mismeasure. Suppose you fill your measuring cup level full—right from the package. How much flour would you have? Just a cup, you think? Let's look at the illustrations on page 18 and see.

What makes this difference between sifted and unsifted flour? It is caused by a peculiar tendency that flour has—the tendency to pack. And the finer the flour, the *more* it packs. Swans Down Cake Flour is so fine that it is important to sift it once before measuring.

1. Start by measuring one level cup of unsifted flour

2. Place flour in a sifter and sift it through once

3. Then pile lightly back into cup —it's more than full

4. Level off the cup. You have left ¼ to ½ cup flour

The woman who is "too busy to bother to sift" may easily put an extra cup of flour into a cake—and ruin it! The recipes in this book call for *sifted flour*. ALWAYS SIFT FLOUR ONCE BEFORE MEASURING.

Measure flour this way (see illustration on page 19). For a cup, pile the sifted flour *lightly* into cup with a scoop or spoon; level off the top with spatula or straight edge of a knife. For a fraction of a cup, cut surface of sifted flour gently toward fraction line with edge of scoop or spoon; do not press it down. For ¼ cup flour, it is easier to measure its equivalent—4 level tablespoons.

Two don'ts about measuring flour. Don't dip up the sifted flour with the cup—it packs it down again. Don't jar the cup on the table or rap it with a spoon while measuring—it causes the flour to settle.

Penalties of too much flour. If your cakes have ever humped in the middle, had a cracked, tough crust, or been dry and compact, you have probably used too much flour. Excessive flour is often, too, the cause of tough pie crust and humped, tunneled muffins.

Baking Powder—Little . . . but Mighty!

Baking powder requires very *special* care in measuring. A tiny bit over or under the given amount brings all sorts of unhappy results in baking. The most frequent error is overmeasurement.

18

Remember that all baking powders are not alike in their action, or in the quantities required for success. Each type of baking powder has an ideal proportion which gives its best results.

All the recipes in this book are built on Calumet, the Double-Acting Baking Powder of the combination type. They need Calumet's Double-Action for perfect results. The amount of baking powder called for may seem small compared to that used for many other baking powders, but the efficiency of Calumet's Double-Action makes this economical proportion possible. One level teaspoon of Calumet Baking Powder to a cup of sifted flour is the usual proportion.

Measuring flour—I cup, and ¾ cup sifted flour

Measuring baking powder—just a level teaspoon

Measuring sugar—brown sugar is firmly packed

Measuring shortening—by cup, spoon, or weight

Measuring liquid—set the cup on a level table

Measuring syrup—fill the spoon, do not dip it

To *measure baking powder,* use a standard measuring spoon. Fill it heaping full, then level off as directed on paper seal of Calumet can, or with straight edge of knife. (See illustration on page 19.)

Don't measure baking powder this way. Don't heap the teaspoon, for a heaping teaspoon may be 3 or 4 level teaspoons. Don't level off the spoon against the side of the can; the rounded edge gives you a rounding, and not a level teaspoon. Don't fill the spoon "about right" and shake off the excess; use your spatula to level off. Don't guess at fractions; use the small sizes of your set of measuring spoons to measure ¼- or ½-teaspoon amounts.

Penalties of too much or too little baking powder. Too much baking powder brings all kinds of woe: batter running over edges of the pan; cake falling in the center; crackled, gummy, tough crust; coarse, crumbly texture. And too little leavening may cause undersized products; peaked, dull crust; heaviness; leathery streaks.

Measuring Sugar, Shortening, and Liquids

Measuring rules for white and brown sugar. (See illustration on page 19.) For granulated or white sugar, fill the cup and level off with spatula or straight edge of knife. Never heap the cup or "scant" it even a little bit! For sugar, too, has baking tragedies to answer for, such as sugary crust, tough texture, and heaviness. Brown sugar takes a very different measuring rule from white. Pack it into the cup so firmly that it will keep the shape of cup when turned out.

Three measuring methods for solid shortening. (See illustration on page 19.) Print butter may be measured by dividing the pound: 1 pound butter equals 2 cups. If you get butter already divided into quarters, remember that each quarter is exactly ½ cup of butter. Shortening in bulk may be measured in small quantities by tablespoon: 4 level tablespoons equals ¼ cup. Pack the shortening firmly into the tablespoon and level off with spatula or straight edge of knife. Measure larger quantities of bulk shortening by cup; pack the shortening in so firmly that it will hold the shape of the cup when turned out and level top with spatula or straight edge of knife. For fraction of cup, press shortening in cup level with fraction mark.

How to measure melted shortening. First melt shortening over hot water. Then measure by level tablespoons.

Measure liquids on a level table. (See illustration on page 19.) A cup of liquid is all that the cup will hold. Set the cup on a level table while you fill it. Don't hold it in your hand. The surface of the liquid may slant and deceive you.

Thick, sticky liquids or syrups, such as molasses, corn syrup, or honey, should be poured into spoon from the container or another spoon. (See illustration on page 19.) Don't dip the spoon into sticky liquids to measure. Too much will cling to under side of spoon.

Cream cake and crisscross pie,
muffins and coconut tea strips — made in a morning.
This is making the most of your time, fuel, and effort

Make a plan for your baking day

MEASURING TABLE

Practical Weights and Measures

4 ounces	¼ pound
16 ounces	1 pound
60 drops	1 teaspoon
3 teaspoons	1 tablespoon
4 tablespoons	¼ cup
8 tablespoons	½ cup
16 tablespoons	1 cup
1 gill	½ cup
2 cups	1 pint
4 cups	2 pints or 1 quart
A dash	less than ⅛ teaspoon

Weights and Measures of Ingredients

FOOD	UNIT	EQUIVALENT
Butter	1 pound	2 cups
	1 ounce	2 tablespoons
Chocolate	1 ounce	1 square
Corn meal	1 pound	3 cups
Currants	1 pound	3 cups
Eggs	1 medium	2 ounces
	8 to 10 medium	1 pound
	8 to 10 egg whites	1 cup
	12 to 14 egg yolks	1 cup
Flour		
Wheat, sifted		
Swans Down	1 pound	4½ cups
Ordinary flour	1 pound	4 cups
Graham	1 pound	3½ cups
Rye	1 pound	5 cups
Lemon, juice	1 medium	3 tablespoons
rind, grated	1 medium	1½ teaspoons
Marshmallows	¼ pound	16 marshmallows
Nuts, in shell		
Almonds	1 pound	2 cups nut meats
Pecans	1 pound	2 cups nut meats
Walnuts	1 pound	2 cups nut meats
All nut meats	¼ pound (4 ounces)	1 cup meats, chopped
Orange, juice	1 medium	½ cup
rind, grated	1 medium	1 tablespoon
Raisins, seeded	1 package (15 ounces)	3¼ cups
seedless	1 package (15 ounces)	3 cups
Sugar		
Brown	1 pound	2 to 2¼ cups, firmly packed
Confectioners'	1 pound	3½ cups
Granulated	1 pound	2¼ cups
Powdered	1 pound	2½ cups

An assortment of pans for every baking need

Pans . . . Oven . . . Proper Cooling
Those Last Important Steps

✿

A PERFECT batter will make a perfect cake only when it is baked correctly. A thick, deep batter and one that is spread out thin present two different baking problems—they require different oven temperatures and baking times.

Use the type of pan specified in the recipe. All the recipes in this book are carefully calculated as to yield, and the baking directions are exactly right for the type and size of pan indicated. There are illustrated above various types of pans, each designed to do justice to various classes of mixtures: butter cake pans—8x8x2-inch pan, 9-inch layer pans, sheet pan, loaf pan; sponge cake or angel food pan; pie plate; muffin pans; fancy cake pans; baking sheet.

Prepare your pans before mixing (see illustration on page 24). The recipes in this book specify whether or not to grease the pan.

Butter is generally preferred for greasing because of the good flavor it imparts to the crust. Melt the butter in a cup over hot water and use only the oil on top. Do not use the salt that sinks to the bottom, as salt tends to make the baked product stick to the pan. A pastry brush is a convenient utensil for greasing. Wash and dry it thoroughly after each using to keep it in good condition.

23

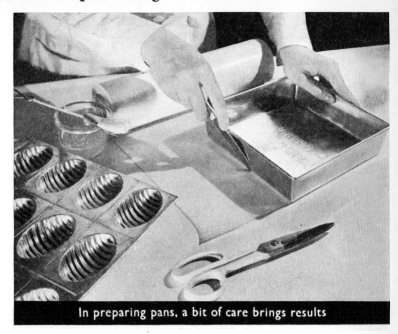

In preparing pans, a bit of care brings results

To prepare pans for large butter cakes, cut paper lining to fit bottom of pan. Grease pan and lining with melted butter. To prepare fancy cake pans, grease bottom of each pan well but sides sparingly. If the sides are too well greased, the little cakes may form rims that bake too brown and spoil their appearance.

Pans for true angel food and sponge cakes should not be greased. If they are greased the batter cannot cling to the sides of the pan as it bakes and thus the cake does not reach its full height. Greasing also causes the cake to fall out of the pan during cooling, making it flat and soggy. When warm, cake of such delicacy is very fragile.

In preparing muffin pans, grease the bottom and sides of each cup well. Fill unused cups half full of water to prevent warping. Iron muffin pans should be heated before greasing. Pie pans never need greasing because pie crust is short enough to grease its own pan. Baking sheets for biscuits and cookies do not need greasing as a rule. The recipes in this book specify greasing when necessary.

Heating the Oven

See that the racks are placed right before the oven gets hot.

Start heating the oven in advance. Heat the oven far enough in advance to have a steady even heat at the right temperature by the time you are ready to begin baking. The nature of your stove must be your guide in deciding when to start heating the oven.

Place pans in oven carefully. Place pans as near the center of the

24

The final test—a cake tester does the trick

oven as possible. Do not place one pan directly over another, and do not crowd the oven full, as it makes uneven baking.

Keep your oven under control. If you know just how to make your oven behave, you have mastered an important part of the art of baking. Keep the oven at the temperature specified in your recipe.

Helps in Controlling Oven Heat

A portable thermometer is a great help in keeping you informed as to just what your oven is doing. It does not control heat, but tells you when to adjust temperature. (See illustration above.)

Many stoves now have oven heat regulators. This is a device that controls the flow of heat and keeps the oven at a steady temperature as long as the heat is on. The oven regulator should be inspected occasionally to make sure that it is registering correctly.

Divide the baking time into quarters. It will help in controlling your oven heat if you know just when you ought to look at your cake and what you may expect to see. For that purpose, baking time for cake has been divided into quarters as follows:

    1st quarter—Cake mixture begins to rise

    2nd quarter—Rising continues; surface begins to brown

    3rd quarter—Finishes rising; continues browning

    4th quarter—Finishes baking; shrinks from sides of pan.

Take a look at your cake at the end of each quarter and, if you find that it is not baking according to this schedule, adjust the heat.

Turn out butter cakes after slight cooling

Oven Temperatures and Baking Time

A range of degrees is covered in baking temperatures. The terms "slow," "moderate," "hot," and "very hot," as applied to oven temperature, cover the generally accepted range which follows:

Slow oven....250° F. to 350° F.   Moderate oven.350° F. to 400° F.
Hot oven......400° F. to 450° F.   Very hot oven..450° F. to 500° F.

Practical oven temperature tests may be made which correspond to these thermometer ranges. Set a pan sprinkled with flour in the oven and if the flour becomes a delicate brown in five minutes, the oven is slow (250° F. to 350° F.). If the flour turns a medium golden brown in five minutes, the oven is moderate (350° F. to 400° F.). If the flour turns a deep dark brown in five minutes, the oven is hot (400° F. to 450° F.). If the flour turns a deep dark brown in three minutes, the oven is very hot (450° F. to 500° F.). These same tests may also be done with white tissue paper or white unglazed paper.

When your oven temperature is exactly that specified in the recipe, your cake should be done in the time given. But to be on the safe side, always test your cake before removing it from the oven. Here are several tests or indications to help you. If cake is done, it should have risen to its full height and have a delicate brown crust. It should have shrunk slightly from sides of pan. The surface of the cake, when pressed lightly by finger, should spring back and leave no imprint. A wire cake tester inserted in center of cake should come out clean and dry. (See illustration, page 25.)

Let sponge cake cool in pan; then remove

Care after Baking

Butter cakes—cool on rack. After removal from the oven, place cake on a rack and let it remain in the pan about 5 minutes. Then loosen from sides with spatula and turn out of pan. Remove paper from bottom of cake and turn right side up on rack to finish cooling. (See illustration on opposite page.)

Sponge cakes—cool in pan. When angel food cake or sponge cake is removed from the oven, turn the pan upside down on a cake rack and let the cake hang in the pan for 1 hour, or until cold. Do not leave it in the pan too long for it may stick, or the crust may roll off in balls. But . . . *don't remove while warm.* The cell walls of angel food cake or sponge cake are so delicate that the cake cannot hold up its own weight until stiffened slightly by cooling. The Swans Down angel food pan is ideal for all types of sponge cakes. Its extended tube and movable slides provide for circulation of air while the cake cools, crisping the crust nicely.

When cake is cold, turn pan right side up. Loosen sides first; insert spatula between cake and sides of pan until tip touches bottom, and press gently against sides of pan, cutting away clinging cake. (See the illustration above.) Loosen the cake around center tube, cutting with slender knife or cake tester. If Swans Down pan is used, loosen cake from bottom of pan by inserting spatula through slots and sliding it across bottom of pan. To remove the cake, tilt the pan and gently draw cake out onto rack.

27

TIME-TABLE FOR BAKING

FOOD	TEMPERATURE	TIME
Cakes		
Angel food cake	275° F.	30 minutes, and then 325° F. 30 minutes or more
Cup cakes	350° to 375° F.	20 to 25 minutes
Fruit cake	250° to 300° F.	1½ to 4 hours
Gingerbread	350° F.	45 to 50 minutes
Jelly roll and sheet cake	400° F.	12 to 15 minutes
*Layer cake		
¾ to 1 inch thick ...	375° F.	20 to 30 minutes
*Loaf cake		
1½ to 2½ inches thick	350° F.	40 to 50 minutes
Over 2½ inches thick	350° F.	1 hour or more
Pound cake	275° to 325° F.	1 to 2 hours
Sponge cake	325° F.	1 hour or more
Cookies		
Most cookies	350° to 425° F.	5 to 15 minutes
Fruit, soft molasses,		
and chocolate cookies	325° to 350° F.	8 to 15 minutes
Meringue		
For pies with cooked		
fillings	350° F.	15 minutes
Pastry		
Pie shells	450° F.	15 minutes
Tart shells	450° F.	10 to 15 minutes
Pies		
Berry and Fruit	425° to 450° F.	15 minutes, and then 350° F. 20 to 30 minutes
(Canned and fresh)		
Custard	450° F.	20 minutes, and then 350° F. 15 minutes
(Uncooked mixture		
baked in uncooked		
pastry)		
Dried fruit	425° F.	10 minutes, and then 350° F. 30 minutes
Quick Breads		
Baking powder biscuits	450° F.	12 to 15 minutes
Coffee cake	400° F.	25 to 30 minutes
Corn bread	425° F.	40 minutes
Fruit or nut bread	350° F.	1 to 1¼ hours
Muffins	400° to 450° F.	25 to 30 minutes
Rolls	425° to 450° F.	15 to 20 minutes

*—Except chocolate cake, which is usually baked about 25° F. lower.

23 Easy Picture Lessons—
The Keys to Baking Success

☼

IN the beginning of this book a large promise was made. You were told that you could gain command of the art of baking through the mastery of a few recipes. It was hinted, too, that these few recipes would be given in such fashion that you could not help but master them easily.

Now comes the test of that promise. In the pages which follow, you will find 23 basic recipes. The basic recipes constitute a series of carefully planned lessons, covering all types of baked products, from the homely pancake or corn bread to the most sumptuous of party cakes. Each basic recipe has a method more or less its own— each teaches you how to make a whole group of recipes, similar in method. These 23 basic recipes are the keys to baking success.

Much as these lessons tell you, they are amazingly easy to understand. Step by step, each is explained, and then illustrated so plainly that you seem to be looking directly into the mixing bowl.

You may wonder, at first glance, why in one lesson the creaming of the butter has been made a feature; in another, the beating of egg yolks; in a third, some detail of handling a cake after baking. But as you study and use the lessons, the plan behind their organization becomes plain. The points chosen for emphasis and illustration are carefully selected with two purposes in mind. They give you, one by one, close-ups of mixing technics particularly important to this or that mixture, and at the same time build a progressive, complete story of the mixing and baking processes common to all the recipes in the book.

So turn now to Basic Recipe 1 (pages 32 and 33) which begins these lessons on mixing and baking. See, for example, how crystal clear this lesson makes the mixing of a one-egg butter cake. Next, as you turn the page, you come upon Chocolate Fudge Loaf, or Basic Recipe 2, with its step-by-step directions and pictures. Turn the page again, and you will find a full page of supporting or similar recipes for each of the two preceding basic recipes (pages 36 and 37). In this way the 23 basic recipe lessons and their groups of similar recipes are arranged throughout the section.

The lessons in this book give you a new understanding of baking. They show why, when quality is all-important, you mix a butter cake one way, and quite another when time is at a premium . . . just how long to beat egg whites for angel food . . . how to give flakiness to biscuits . . . make muffins without tunnels . . . perfect pastry, proud meringues. Here is the way to beat the world at baking!

These Basic Recipes
Teach Butter Cakes and Cookies

☼

THE chart below gives the basic recipes for butter cakes and cookies and shows the relationship between these basic recipes, each representing a type of mixture, and other recipes in the book.

BASIC RECIPE	DESCRIPTION	RECIPES SIMILAR TO BASIC RECIPE
1. Calumet One-egg Cake (page 32)	Simplest version of butter cake	Raisin Cup Cakes Boston Cream Pie Nut Loaf Cake Harvest Cake Golden Spice Cake *(Recipes on page 36)*
2. Chocolate Fudge Loaf (page 34)	A simple butter cake with chocolate added	Chocolate Marshmallow Loaf Chocolate Cup Cakes Silhouette Cake *(Recipes on page 37)*
3. Coconut Layer Cake (page 38)	The standard butter cake	Southern Spanish Cake Ribbon Cake Burnt Sugar Cake *(Recipes on page 42)*
4. Economical Gold Cake (page 40)	Butter cake made with egg yolks	Golden Anniversary Cake Little Baltimore Cakes Gold Cake *(Recipes on page 43)*
5. Lady Baltimore Cake (page 44)	Butter cake made with egg whites	Silver Cake White Moon Cake Frosted Marble Cake *(Recipes on page 48)*
6. Caramel Devil's Food (page 46)	Butter cake of the rich, sweet, chocolate type	Sour Cream Devil's Food Prize Devil's Food Cake Ambassador Cake *(Recipes on page 49)*
7. Busy Day Cake (page 50)	Butter cake made by the jiffy-quick method	Calumet Quick Cake Creole Tier Cake Aladdin Chocolate Cake Quick Spice Cake *(Recipes on page 54)*
8. Small Cakes (page 52)	Some little tricks with butter cake	Walnut Cream Cakes Ginger Tea Cakes Orange Tea Cakes *(Recipes on page 55)*
9. Date Surprises (page 56)	Filled cookies from rolled cooky dough	Sugar Cookies Sand Tarts Butterscotch Cookies *(Recipes on page 60)*
10. Vanilla Nut Cookies (page 58)	Ice box cookies always on hand	Peanut Butter Cookies Chocolate Walnut Dollars Coconut Ice Box Cookies Chocolate Pin Wheels *(Recipes on page 61)*

Plain or fancy, light or dark,
silver, gold, or ribbon cake, made in layers or loaves —
you will master them all with these picture lessons

The popular butter cake family

31

CALUMET ONE-EGG CAKE

2 cups sifted Swans Down Cake Flour
2 teaspoons Calumet Baking Powder
¼ teaspoon salt   4 tablespoons butter or other shortening
1 cup sugar   1 egg, unbeaten   ¾ cup milk   1 teaspoon vanilla

Sift flour once, measure, add baking powder and salt, and
sift together three times. Cream butter thoroughly, add sugar
gradually, creaming together until blended and light. Add egg
and beat very thoroughly. Add flour, alternately with milk, a
small amount at a time. Beat after each addition until smooth.
Add vanilla. Bake in a greased pan, 8x8x2 inches, in moderate oven (350° F.) 50 minutes. Spread Clever Judy Frosting
(page 108) on top and sides of cake. Or bake in two greased
8-inch layer pans, or greased cup-cake pans in moderate oven
(375° F.) 25 minutes, or until done.

Basic Recipe 1

KEY STEPS

1 How to sift ingredients
2 How to cream butter and sugar together for cake
3 How to add whole egg, *beaten or unbeaten*, to well-creamed mixture
4 How to add flour, milk

1 Measure the sifted flour, baking powder, and salt into sifter.
Then sift these dry ingredients together three times. This sepa-
rates the tiny particles of Swans Down Cake Flour and thoroughly
blends them with the baking powder and salt. Raise the sifter to let
the flour pile up lightly, but not so high that it packs as it falls. It is
convenient to use two squares of paper in sifting.

☼

2 "Cream" the butter by working it against the sides of the bowl
with the back of a mixing paddle or wooden spoon. When the
butter is soft and smooth and very light in color, add about 2 tablespoons sugar, and cream well. Continue in this manner until all
sugar is added and mixture is creamed to a fluffy lightness.

☼

3 In this cake the egg may be added beaten or unbeaten. We find it
simpler to drop the unbeaten egg right into the creamed butter
and sugar and then beat *vigorously*. This spirited beating is especially important when the egg is not beaten first. Lift the mixture up
as you beat to enclose as much air as possible. Continue beating until egg is thoroughly blended and mixture is light and smooth.

☼

4 The manner of adding the flour and milk is important. Add about
¼ of the flour, first stirring gently round and round, and then
beating until the mixture is smooth. Next add about ⅓ of the milk in
the same way. Continue until all flour and milk are used. Begin and
end with flour to prevent curdling. Keep batter low in bowl.

Simplest method of mixing butter cake

*Cup cakes, loaf cake,
layer cake
all from one recipe*

1. Sift flour, baking powder, and salt three times

2. Work butter with paddle or spoon until soft

3. Add unbeaten egg and beat mixture vigorously

4. Add flour and milk alternately in small amounts

In this method, as shown in the four pictures above, the butter and sugar are creamed well, the whole egg is added beaten or unbeaten, and the flour and liquid are added alternately

33

CHOCOLATE FUDGE LOAF

2 cups sifted Swans Down Cake Flour
2 teaspoons Calumet Baking Powder
½ teaspoon salt   ½ cup butter or other shortening
1 cup sugar   1 egg, well beaten
2 squares Baker's Unsweetened Chocolate, melted
¾ cup milk   1 teaspoon vanilla

Sift flour once, measure, add baking powder and salt, and sift together three times. Cream butter thoroughly, add sugar gradually, and cream together until light and fluffy. Add egg and beat well; then add chocolate. Blend. Add flour, alternately with milk, a small amount at a time. Beat after each addition until smooth. Add vanilla. Bake in a greased pan, 8x8x2 inches, in moderate oven (325° F.) 1 hour. Spread Fudge Frosting (page 108) on top and sides of cake. *Basic Recipe 2*

KEY STEPS

1 How to melt chocolate easily over hot water
2 How to add beaten egg
3 How to blend chocolate completely with mixture
4 How to bake a chocolate cake batter correctly

1 Always melt chocolate over hot water—never over direct heat—as it scorches very easily. For this purpose use any utensil that fits into the top of the tea kettle, or a small double boiler. It is not necessary to cut the squares of chocolate in pieces first, although chocolate melts more quickly when this is done.

☼

2 In this cake the egg is added *beaten*. Choose the smallest bowl your egg beater will fit into, then beat the egg until it is light and foamy. Pour the well-beaten egg over the creamed butter and sugar mixture and blend. Stir gently at first, then beat until the mixture is light and puffy.

☼

3 Melted chocolate may be most thoroughly blended with other ingredients by adding it to the creamed mixture. Be sure to blend the chocolate perfectly. Watch the fluffy, cream-colored mass become streaked with the reddish brown of the chocolate, then as you continue beating see it turn into a smooth, evenly colored chocolate mixture. The batter is now ready for the final ingredients.

☼

4 The baking temperature is a little lower (about 25° F.) for chocolate cake than for plain butter cakes. Remember that chocolate scorches very easily because it is high in fat. Try to control the heat of your oven so that by the time the batter is in the pan, the temperature will remain at 325° F. during the entire baking period.

Adding chocolate to a simple butter cake

Such good chocolate cake so easily made becomes a menu standby

1. Chocolate is melted over water to prevent scorching

2. Beat egg; add to creamed mixture and mix well

3. Blend chocolate with butter, sugar, and egg mixture

4. Bake chocolate cake at slightly lower temperature

The chocolate should be melted over hot water, added to the creamed butter, sugar, and egg mixture, and blended. Note the lower baking temperature used for chocolate cake

35

RAISIN CUP CAKES

Use recipe for Calumet One-egg Cake (page 32). Pour batter into greased cup-cake pans, filling them ⅔ full. Sprinkle seedless raisins over tops of cakes. Bake in moderate oven (375° F.) 20 minutes, or until done. Makes 24.

☼

BOSTON CREAM PIE

Use recipe for Calumet One-egg Cake (page 32). Bake in two greased 9-inch layer pans in moderate oven (375° F.) 25 minutes. Spread Custard Cream Filling (page 74) between layers. Sift powdered sugar over top.

☼

NUT LOAF CAKE

Use recipe for Calumet One-egg Cake (page 32), adding 1 cup chopped walnut meats to cake mixture after egg has been added. Bake in greased pan, 8x8x2 inches, in a moderate oven (350° F.) 50 minutes, or until done. Spread Clever Judy Frosting (page 108) on top and sides of cake.

☼

HARVEST CAKE
(2 egg yolks)

2 cups sifted Swans Down Cake Flour   2 teaspoons Calumet Baking Powder
¼ teaspoon salt   ⅓ cup butter or other shortening
¾ cup brown sugar, firmly packed
2 egg yolks, unbeaten   ⅔ cup milk   1 teaspoon vanilla

Sift flour once, measure, add baking powder and salt, and sift together three times. Cream butter thoroughly, add sugar gradually, and cream together until light and fluffy. Add egg yolks; beat well. Add flour, alternately with milk, a small amount at a time. Beat after each addition until smooth. Add vanilla. Bake in a greased pan, 8x8x2 inches, in moderate oven (350° F.) 45 minutes, or until done. Spread Harvest Moon Frosting (page 106) on top and sides of cake.

☼

GOLDEN SPICE CAKE
(1 egg or 2 egg yolks)

2 cups sifted Swans Down Cake Flour   2½ teaspoons Calumet Baking Powder
¼ teaspoon salt   1 teaspoon cinnamon   ¼ teaspoon cloves
¼ teaspoon nutmeg   ¼ teaspoon mace   ½ teaspoon allspice
4 tablespoons butter or other shortening   ¾ cup brown sugar, firmly packed
1 egg (or 2 egg yolks), well beaten   ¾ cup milk

Sift flour once, measure, add baking powder, salt, and spices, and sift together three times. Cream butter, add sugar gradually, and cream together thoroughly. Add egg, then flour, alternately with milk, a small amount at a time. Beat after each addition until smooth. Bake in a greased pan, 8x8x2 inches, in moderate oven (350° F.) 50 minutes. Spread Butter Frosting (page 107) on top and sides of cake, if desired.

CHOCOLATE MARSHMALLOW LOAF

Use recipe for Chocolate Fudge Loaf (page 34). Turn cake from pan, and while still warm, cover bottom with marshmallows that have been rinsed with cold water and cut in halves crosswise. When cake is almost cold, cover with Hungarian Chocolate Frosting and Filling (page 108).

☼

CHOCOLATE CUP CAKES
(2 eggs)

1½ cups sifted Swans Down Cake Flour   1½ teaspoons Calumet Baking Powder
½ teaspoon salt   ⅓ cup butter or other shortening   1 cup sugar
2 eggs, well beaten   2 squares Baker's Unsweetened Chocolate, melted
½ cup milk   1 teaspoon vanilla

Sift flour once, measure, add baking powder and salt, and sift together three times. Cream butter thoroughly, add sugar gradually, and cream together until light and fluffy. Add eggs and beat well; then add chocolate. Blend. Add flour, alternately with milk, a small amount at a time. Beat after each addition until smooth. Add vanilla. Pour into greased cup-cake pans, filling them ⅔ full. Bake in moderate oven (350° F.) 20 minutes, or until done. Cover with Harvest Moon Frosting (page 106), or with Seven Minute Frosting (page 104) and chopped nuts. Makes 20 cup cakes.

☼

SILHOUETTE CAKE
(1 egg and 2 egg yolks)

2⅓ cups sifted Swans Down Cake Flour   2¼ teaspoons Calumet Baking Powder
¼ teaspoon salt   ½ cup butter or other shortening   1 cup sugar
1 egg and 2 egg yolks, well beaten   ¾ cup milk   1 teaspoon vanilla

For chocolate mixture

2½ squares Baker's Unsweetened Chocolate, melted   ½ teaspoon soda
3 tablespoons sugar   2 tablespoons melted butter
¼ teaspoon salt   ¼ cup boiling water

Sift flour once, measure, add baking powder and salt, and sift together three times. Cream butter thoroughly, add sugar gradually, and cream together until light and fluffy. Add egg and egg yolks and beat well. Prepare chocolate mixture by combining melted chocolate, soda, sugar, butter, salt, and water, and mix well. Add flour to light mixture, alternately with milk, a small amount at a time. Mix thoroughly after each addition. Add vanilla. Pour one-third of batter into greased 8-inch layer pan. Add chocolate mixture to remaining batter, blend, and pour into two greased 8-inch layer pans. Bake in moderate oven (375° F.) 20 minutes, or until done.

To frost cake, arrange light layer between dark layers, spread each layer and sides of cake with Harvest Moon Frosting (double recipe, page 106), omitting nuts. Pile frosting on top. Cool. Melt 2 additional squares Baker's Unsweetened Chocolate with 2 teaspoons butter. When frosting is set, pour chocolate mixture over cake, letting it run down on sides.

COCONUT LAYER CAKE

2 cups sifted Swans Down Cake Flour
2 teaspoons Calumet Baking Powder
½ teaspoon salt   ⅔ cup butter or other shortening   1 cup sugar
3 egg yolks, well beaten   ⅓ cup milk   1 teaspoon vanilla
3 egg whites, stiffly beaten   1 can Baker's Coconut, Southern Style

Sift flour once, measure, add baking powder and salt, and sift together three times. Cream butter thoroughly, add sugar gradually, and cream together until light and fluffy. Add egg yolks; then flour, alternately with milk, a small amount at a time. Beat after each addition until smooth. Add vanilla and fold in egg whites. Bake in two greased 9-inch layer pans in moderate oven (375° F.) 25 to 30 minutes. Spread Seven Minute Frosting (page 104) over cake; sprinkle with coconut. Double recipe for three 10-inch layers.   *Basic Recipe 3*

KEY STEPS

1 How to cream butter and sugar mixture carefully

2 How to beat yolks and whites of eggs *separately*

3 How to beat the batter

4 When and how to fold in the beaten egg whites

1 Let butter stand at room temperature a short time so that it may be worked easily and quickly. After the butter is creamed until soft and waxy, add sugar, about 2 tablespoons at a time, beating well after each addition. Finally, beat mixture until it is fluffy and light.

☼

2 Separate yolks and whites of eggs. Beat yolks until thick with rotary egg beater; then add to creamed mixture. Note the thick, continuous stream in which the well-beaten egg yolks fall. With a mixing paddle or wooden spoon, beat the egg yolks into the creamed butter and sugar until mixture is smooth, light, and fluffy.

☼

3 After all the flour and liquid have been added alternately and thoroughly blended, your batter should look like this—thick, but very smooth and fluffy. Give the batter a few final strokes after the flavoring is added, for whenever stiffly beaten egg whites are to be folded into a batter, all beating is done *before* the whites are added.

☼

4 A critical step this. Beat egg whites until stiff with rotary egg beater or whisk. Pile them lightly on top of batter. Cut down through entire mixture with mixing paddle or wooden spoon, then lift up the yellow batter and fold it gently over the glistening whites. Continue until no particle of egg white can be seen. Work quickly to retain enclosed air, yet thoroughly to blend egg whites and avoid risk of large holes in finished cake.

Standard method of mixing butter cake

Any table . . . . any day
seems festive
if coconut cake appears

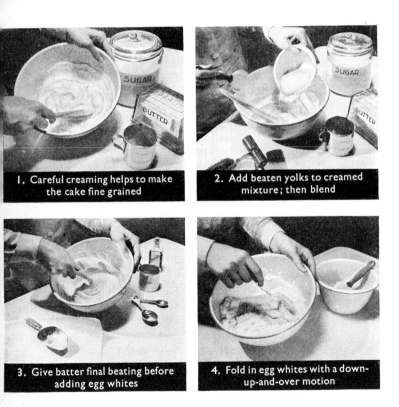

1. Careful creaming helps to make the cake fine grained

2. Add beaten yolks to creamed mixture; then blend

3. Give batter final beating before adding egg whites

4. Fold in egg whites with a down-up-and-over motion

Here, the egg yolks and egg whites are beaten separately. The egg yolks are added to the well-creamed butter and sugar; the egg whites gently folded in as the last step in mixing

ECONOMICAL GOLD CAKE

2 cups sifted Swans Down Cake Flour
2 teaspoons Calumet Baking Powder
½ cup butter or other shortening   1 cup sugar
3 egg yolks, beaten until thick and lemon-colored   ¾ cup milk
1 teaspoon vanilla or ½ teaspoon orange extract

Sift flour once, measure, add baking powder, and sift together three times. Cream butter thoroughly, add sugar gradually and cream together until light and fluffy. Add egg yolks and beat well; then flour, alternately with milk, a small amount at a time. Beat after each addition until smooth. Add flavoring. Beat well. Bake in a greased pan, 8x8x2 inches, in moderate oven (350° F.) 50 minutes, or until done. Spread Luscious Lemon Frosting (page 107) over cake. Double recipe for two square layers as pictured on page 41.

Basic Recipe 4

KEY STEPS

1 How to beat egg yolks correctly for gold cake

2 How to add beaten egg yolks to creamed mixture

3 How to beat in air to make batter very light

4 How to fill the cake pan

1 You cannot be too particular about the beating of egg yolks for gold cake. The air beaten into them has a great deal to do with making the cake light. Use a rotary beater and a bowl suited in size to the number of egg yolks to be beaten. Notice the changing appearance of the yolks as you beat. Watch them grow lighter in color as more and more air is enclosed.

☼

2 Coax the thick, fluffy mass of egg yolks out of the bowl with rubber scraper or spatula. Then *beat* the yolks into the thoroughly creamed butter and sugar. Note how the mixture becomes velvety smooth and delicately light as it increases in volume. The additional air beaten in at this stage helps to lighten the cake.

☼

3 Last—and very important—is the final beating of the batter. This last beating of all the ingredients together thoroughly blends them and incorporates still more air. Up and over—up and over—goes the mixing paddle, enclosing air with each stroke. Watch the batter take on a lighter color and a soft sunny sheen. Note also how light and smooth it has become.

☼

4 See how the batter falls in ribbonlike folds as it is poured into the pan. Spread batter uniformly and smoothly, pushing it up against the sides and into the corners of the pan so that the cake will have an even surface and may rise evenly.

A butter cake which uses egg yolks only

*Cuts well and stays moist
—this gold cake
with its lemon frosting*

1. Beat egg yolks until thick and light and lemon yellow

2. Beat the fluffy egg yolks into creamed butter and sugar

3. A final hard beating makes the batter smooth and light

4. Spread the batter smoothly and evenly in a greased pan

The beating of egg yolks, blending them with creamed butter and sugar, and final beating of the batter, after all ingredients are combined, are important points in making this cake

41

Other Recipes Made Like Coconut Layer Cake

See Basic Recipe 3, Page 38

SOUTHERN SPANISH CAKE
(2 eggs)

1¾ cups sifted Swans Down Cake Flour   1½ teaspoons Calumet Baking Powder
¼ teaspoon salt   1 teaspoon cinnamon   ½ cup butter or other shortening
1 cup sugar   2 egg yolks, well beaten   ½ cup milk
2 egg whites, stiffly beaten

Sift flour once, measure, add baking powder, salt, and cinnamon, and sift together three times. Cream butter thoroughly, add sugar gradually, and cream together until light and fluffy. Add egg yolks, and beat well; then add flour, alternately with milk, a small amount at a time. Mix thoroughly after each addition. Fold in egg whites. Bake in two greased 8-inch layer pans in moderate oven (375° F.) 25 minutes. Spread Coffee Frosting (page 109) between layers and on top and sides of cake.

✿

RIBBON CAKE
(3 eggs)

3 cups sifted Swans Down Cake Flour   3 teaspoons Calumet Baking Powder
⅔ cup butter or other shortening   1½ cups sugar   3 egg yolks, well beaten
1 cup milk   3 egg whites, stiffly beaten   ¾ teaspoon cinnamon
⅛ teaspoon cloves   ¼ teaspoon mace   ¼ teaspoon nutmeg
1½ tablespoons molasses   ⅓ cup raisins, finely cut   ⅓ cup figs, finely cut

Sift flour once, measure, add baking powder, and sift together three times. Cream butter thoroughly, add sugar gradually, and cream together until light and fluffy. Add egg yolks and beat well. Add flour, alternately with milk, a small amount at a time. Beat after each addition until smooth. Fold in egg whites. Fill two greased 9-inch layer pans with two-thirds of mixture. To remaining mixture, add spices, molasses, and fruit, and pour into one greased 9-inch layer pan. Bake layers in moderate oven (375° F.) minutes. Arrange spice layer between light layers. Spread currant jelly between layers and Seven Minute Frosting (page 104) on top and sides of cake.

✿

BURNT SUGAR CAKE
(3 eggs)

½ cup sugar   ¼ cup hot water   3 cups sifted Swans Down Cake Flour
3 teaspoons Calumet Baking Powder   ½ teaspoon salt
½ cup butter or other shortening   1½ cups sugar   3 egg yolks, well beaten
1 cup water   1 teaspoon vanilla
2 tablespoons caramelized sugar syrup   3 egg whites, stiffly beaten

To make caramelized sugar syrup, place ½ cup sugar in skillet over medium flame and stir constantly until melted and quite dark. Remove from fire, add ¼ cup hot water, and stir until dissolved. Cool.

Sift flour once, measure, add baking powder and salt; sift together three times. Cream butter thoroughly, add sugar gradually, and cream together until light and fluffy. Add egg yolks and beat well. Add flour, alternately with water, a small amount at a time. Beat after each addition until smooth. Add vanilla. Add 2 tablespoons caramelized sugar syrup. Blend. Fold in egg whites. Bake in two greased 9-inch layer pans in moderate oven (375° F.) 25 minutes. Spread with Burnt Sugar Frosting (page 106).

42

GOLDEN ANNIVERSARY CAKE

(5 egg yolks and 2 egg whites)

4 cups sifted Swans Down Cake Flour   4 teaspoons Calumet Baking Powder
1 cup butter   2 cups sugar   5 egg yolks, beaten until thick and lemon-colored
1⅓ cups milk   ½ teaspoon lemon extract
2 egg whites, stiffly beaten

Sift flour once, measure, add baking powder, and sift together three times. Cream butter thoroughly, add sugar gradually, and cream together until light and fluffy. Add egg yolks and beat well. Add flour, alternately with milk, a small amount at a time. Beat after each addition until smooth. Add lemon extract. Fold in egg whites. Bake in four greased 9-inch layer pans in a moderate oven (350° F.) 25 minutes. Spread Lemon Seven Minute Frosting (page 106) between layers and on top and sides of cake.

✿

LITTLE BALTIMORE CAKES

(4 egg yolks)

1 cup sifted Swans Down Cake Flour   1 teaspoon Calumet Baking Powder
⅛ teaspoon salt   1 tablespoon grated orange rind
4 tablespoons butter or other shortening   ½ cup sugar
4 egg yolks, well beaten   ¼ cup milk

Sift flour once, measure, add baking powder and salt, and sift together three times. Add orange rind to butter and cream thoroughly. Add sugar gradually and cream together until light and fluffy. Add egg yolks and beat well. Add flour, alternately with milk, a small amount at a time. Beat after each addition until smooth. Bake in deep, well-greased cup-cake pans in moderate oven (375° F.) 25 minutes. Cool. Cut each cake crosswise in three even slices. Put slices together again with Macaroon Filling (page 106). Cover tops and sides with Macaroon Frosting (page 106) and sprinkle with unblanched pistachios, chopped. Makes 15 cakes.

✿

GOLD CAKE

(8 egg yolks)

2¾ cups sifted Swans Down Cake Flour   2¾ teaspoons Calumet Baking Powder
½ teaspoon salt   ¾ cup butter   1¼ cups sugar   8 egg yolks
¾ cup milk   ½ teaspoon lemon extract

Sift flour once, measure, add baking powder and salt, and sift together three times. Cream butter thoroughly, add sugar gradually, and cream together until light and fluffy. Beat egg yolks very thoroughly with rotary egg beater until light colored and thick enough to fall from beater in heavy continuous stream. Add to creamed mixture and beat until very smooth, almost waxy in appearance. Add flour, alternately with milk, a small amount at a time, beating very thoroughly after each addition. When all flour is added, beat thoroughly again. Add lemon extract. Bake in three greased 9-inch layer pans in moderate oven (375° F.) 20 minutes, or until done. Spread Orange Butter Frosting (page 107) between layers and on top of cake. *This cake requires especially thorough beating.*

LADY BALTIMORE CAKE

3 cups sifted Swans Down Cake Flour
3 teaspoons Calumet Baking Powder   ¼ teaspoon salt
½ cup butter or other shortening   1½ cups sugar
½ cup milk   ½ cup water   1 teaspoon vanilla
¼ teaspoon almond extract   3 egg whites, stiffly beaten

Sift flour once, measure, add baking powder and salt, and
sift together three times. Cream butter thoroughly, add sugar
gradually, and cream together until light and fluffy. Add flour,
alternately with liquid, a small amount at a time. Beat after
each addition until smooth. Add flavoring; fold in egg whites.
Bake in two greased 9-inch layer pans in moderate oven (375°
F.) 20 minutes. Spread Lady Baltimore Filling (page 109) between layers and Lady Baltimore Frosting over cake. Double
recipe to make three 10-inch layers.

Basic Recipe 5

KEY STEPS

1 How to cream butter an
   sugar for a fine textur

2 How to blend flour an
   liquid with cake mixtur

3 When and how much t
   beat egg whites for cak

4 How to fold in egg whit

1   Add about 2 tablespoons of sugar to the thoroughly creame
   butter. With back of mixing paddle or wooden spoon work mix
ture until smooth. Continue adding sugar gradually until all is used
creaming until mixture is very light and fluffy. A thorough cream
ing will reward you with an especially fine cake.

☼

2   The combination of milk and water gives better volume and
   whiter, more tender cake than when milk or water alone is used
Use cautious strokes after each addition of liquid to avoid splash
ing; then beat vigorously. For white cake of superior quality, bea
extra hard and long after each addition of flour and liquid.

☼

3   Beat egg whites until they just hold the snowy peaks that form
   when the beater is lifted. Notice how moist and shiny they are
Egg whites beaten beyond this point have less leavening power
also, they break up in dry flakes and make your cake dry.

☼

4   Pile the light fluff of beaten egg whites on top of batter, the
   gently cut down through to bottom of bowl. Lift up some of th
thick batter, and fold it over egg whites, being careful not to brea
any air bubbles. Repeat, in a quick rhythmic down-up-and-ove
motion. Gradually the egg whites are blended and the thick batte
thins to a smooth, silvery white.

Butter cake which uses egg whites only

Velvety crumb, fine grain
—two signs of
any Calumet butter cake

1. Add sugar to soft butter gradually, creaming well

2. Beat hard after each addition of flour and liquid

3. Beat the egg whites only when ready to add to batter

4. Be quick and gentle in folding in egg whites; blend

In this type of cake, it is important that the butter and sugar be creamed very thoroughly. The egg whites are beaten until stiff, but not dry, and folded gently into the batter last

CARAMEL DEVIL'S FOOD CAKE

2 cups sifted Swans Down Cake Flour
1 teaspoon soda   ½ cup butter or other shortening
1¼ cups brown sugar, firmly packed   2 eggs, unbeaten
3 squares Baker's Unsweetened Chocolate, melted
1 cup milk   1 teaspoon vanilla

Sift flour once, measure, add soda, and sift together three times. Cream butter thoroughly, add sugar gradually, and cream together until light and fluffy. Add eggs, one at a time, beating well after each addition. Add chocolate and blend. Add flour, alternately with milk, a small amount at a time. Beat after each addition until smooth. Add vanilla. Bake in two deep greased 9-inch layer pans in moderate oven (350° F.) 25 minutes. Spread with Caramel Frosting (page 109). Double recipe to make three 10-inch layers. *Basic Recipe 6*

KEY STEPS

1 How to add and mix soda
2 How to measure brown sugar for the best results
3 How to add whole eggs unbeaten, to the mixture
4 How and when best to add the melted chocolate

1 That snowy drift falling from the paper is Swans Down Cake Flour and soda. Here soda is used to neutralize the acid in the brown sugar and chocolate, leavening the cake and giving it color. A triple sifting distributes it evenly and removes the tiniest lumps. This is a very simple way of adding soda.

✿

2 Brown sugar adds a special richness of flavor to devil's food. But be wary in measuring it or you will get an inaccurate amount. Press brown sugar tightly into the cup, using the back of a spoon. (See page 20.) Sift it if there are any hard lumps. Add brown sugar gradually to creamed butter and beat thoroughly after each addition.

✿

3 The eggs are added, unbeaten, to the fluffy creamed mixture. Add them, one at a time, stirring carefully round and round, and then beating *hard* until smooth. Vigorous beating is needed to blend each egg thoroughly and to enclose air in mixture. This method of beating in whole eggs is often used when a fine, close-textured cake, such as this rich devil's food, is desired.

✿

4 Add melted chocolate to creamed butter, sugar, and egg mixture and beat well to blend chocolate thoroughly. A rubber scraper is handy for removing the last bit of chocolate from the bowl. Adding chocolate in this manner gives a lighter and finer-grained devil's food than when the chocolate is first cooked with part of the liquid and sugar, and it is a simpler method.

The best way to make devil's food cake

*Use a sharp, strong knife,
rinsed frequently,
for cake wedges like this*

1. Sift soda and flour together
three times to mix

2. Cream butter and brown sugar
until smooth and fluffy

3. Add the unbeaten eggs, singly,
beating mixture hard

4. For best results, add chocolate
to creamed mixture

Melted chocolate is added to butter, sugar, and egg mixture rather than cooked with part of the liquid and sugar and then added. This gives an especially light, fine-grained cake

47

Other Recipes Made Like Lady Baltimore Cake

See Basic Recipe 5, Page 44

SILVER CAKE
(4 egg whites)

3 cups sifted Swans Down Cake Flour	3 teaspoons Calumet Baking Powder
½ cup butter or other shortening	1½ cups sugar 1 cup milk
½ teaspoon lemon extract	4 egg whites, stiffly beaten

Sift flour once, measure, add baking powder, and sift together three times. Cream butter thoroughly, add sugar gradually, and cream together until light and fluffy. Add flour, alternately with milk, a small amount at a time. Beat after each addition until smooth. Add lemon extract. Fold in egg whites and bake in two greased 9-inch layer pans in moderate oven (375° F.) 25 to 30 minutes. Spread Boiled Frosting (page 107) or Seven Minute Frosting (page 104) between layers and on top and sides of cake.

✿

WHITE MOON CAKE
(5 egg whites)

3 cups sifted Swans Down Cake Flour	3 teaspoons Calumet Baking Powder
½ teaspoon salt ⅔ cup butter or other shortening	2 cups sugar
1 cup milk 1 teaspoon vanilla	5 egg whites, stiffly beaten

Sift flour once, measure, add baking powder and salt, and sift together three times. Cream butter thoroughly, add sugar gradually, and cream together until light and fluffy. Add flour, alternately with milk, a small amount at a time. Beat after each addition until smooth. Add vanilla; fold in egg whites. Bake in three greased 9-inch layer pans in slow oven (325° F.) 15 minutes; then increase heat slightly to moderate (350° F.) and bake 15 minutes longer. Spread Luscious Lemon Frosting (page 107) between layers and on top of cake, or spread Lemon Seven Minute Frosting (page 106) thickly between layers and on top and sides of cake.

✿

FROSTED CHOCOLATE MARBLE CAKE
(6 egg whites)

3 cups sifted Swans Down Cake Flour	3 teaspoons Calumet Baking Powder
½ teaspoon salt ¾ cup butter or other shortening	2 cups sugar
¾ cup milk 1 teaspoon vanilla	6 egg whites, stiffly beaten
3 squares Baker's Unsweetened Chocolate, melted	
4 tablespoons sugar ¼ cup boiling water	¼ teaspoon soda

Sift flour once, measure, add baking powder and salt, and sift together three times. Cream butter thoroughly, add sugar gradually, and cream together until light and fluffy. Add flour, alternately with milk, a small amount at a time. Beat after each addition until smooth. Add vanilla. Fold in egg whites. To melted chocolate, add sugar and boiling water, stirring until blended. Then add soda and stir until thickened. Cool slightly. Divide batter into two parts. To one part add chocolate mixture. Put by tablespoons into a greased pan, 10x10x2 inches, alternating light and dark mixtures. Bake in moderate oven (350° F.) 55 minutes, or until done. Spread Chocolate Seven Minute Frosting (page 106) on top and sides of cake.

SOUR CREAM DEVIL'S FOOD CAKE
(1 egg)

2 cups sifted Swans Down Cake Flour
1 teaspoon soda   ½ teaspoon salt   ⅓ cup butter or other shortening
1¼ cups sugar   1 egg, unbeaten
3 squares Baker's Unsweetened Chocolate, melted
1 teaspoon vanilla   ½ cup thick sour cream   ¾ cup sweet milk

Sift flour once, measure, add soda and salt, and sift together three times. Cream butter thoroughly, add sugar gradually, and cream together well. Add egg and beat very thoroughly; then chocolate and vanilla and blend. Add about ¼ of flour and beat well; then add sour cream and beat thoroughly. Add remaining flour, alternately with milk, in small amounts, beating after each addition until smooth. Bake in two greased 9-inch layer pans in moderate oven (350° F.) 30 minutes, or until done. Spread Chocolate Butter Frosting (page 108) between layers and on top of cake.

☼

PRIZE DEVIL'S FOOD CAKE
(3 eggs)

2 cups sifted Swans Down Cake Flour   2¾ teaspoons Calumet Baking Powder
¼ teaspoon salt   ⅔ cup butter or other shortening   1½ cups sugar
3 eggs, well beaten   3 squares Baker's Unsweetened Chocolate, melted
¾ cup milk   1 teaspoon vanilla

Sift flour once, measure, add baking powder and salt, and sift together three times. Cream butter thoroughly, add sugar gradually, and cream together until light and fluffy. Add eggs and beat well. Add chocolate. Blend. Add flour, alternately with milk, a small amount at a time. Beat after each addition until smooth. Add vanilla. Bake in two greased 9-inch layer pans in moderate oven (350° F.) 35 minutes. Spread Seven Minute Frosting (page 104) between layers and on top and sides of cake.

☼

AMBASSADOR CHOCOLATE CAKE
(3 eggs)

2 cups sifted Swans Down Cake Flour   1 teaspoon soda
½ teaspoon salt   1 cup butter or other shortening
1⅓ cups brown sugar, firmly packed   3 eggs, well beaten
4 squares Baker's Unsweetened Chocolate, melted   ⅔ cup water

Sift flour once, measure, add soda and salt, and sift together three times. Cream butter thoroughly, add sugar gradually, and cream together until light and fluffy. Add eggs and beat well. Add chocolate and beat until smooth. Add flour, alternately with water, a small amount at a time. Beat after each addition until smooth. Bake in two deep greased 9-inch layer pans in moderate oven (350° F.) 30 minutes. Spread Seven Minute Frosting (page 104) between layers and on top and sides of cake, piling frosting thickly on top. Melt 2 additional squares Baker's Unsweetened Chocolate with 2 teaspoons butter. When frosting is set, pour chocolate over cake.

BUSY DAY CAKE

3 cups sifted Swans Down Cake Flour

4 teaspoons Calumet Baking Powder   ¼ teaspoon salt

1⅔ cups sugar   ½ cup softened butter or other shortening

3 eggs, well beaten   1¼ cups milk   1 teaspoon vanilla

Sift flour once, measure, add baking powder, salt, and sugar, and sift together three times. Add butter. Combine eggs, milk, and vanilla, and add to flour mixture, stirring until all flour is dampened. Then beat vigorously one minute. Bake in three greased 9-inch layer pans in moderate oven (375° F.) 25 minutes. Spread Creole Butter Frosting (double recipe, page 109) between layers and on top and sides of cake. If desired, flavor cake with ½ teaspoon orange extract or 1 tablespoon grated orange rind; spread orange marmalade between layers and sift powdered sugar over top of cake. *Basic Recipe 7*

KEY STEPS

1 How to sift *all* the dry ingredients at one time

2 How to combine liquids

3 How to combine all cake ingredients very quickly

4 How to handle quick cake after it is baked

1 Into the sifter go all the dry ingredients—Swans Down Cake Flour, Calumet Baking Powder, salt, and sugar. This unusual practice of sifting the sugar with the flour is in the interest of *speed*. Three times the dry ingredients go through the sifter together. The third and last time they are sifted directly into the mixing bowl.

☼

2 To the foamy, well-beaten eggs, add the milk and vanilla, then pour into the flour mixture to which the softened butter has already been added. Melted butter is often used in these quickly mixed cakes, but we find that softened butter gives better results. The butter should not be hard or it does not mix with the other ingredients.

☼

3 Here you see the quickly mixed cake batter in the beginning stage. All the ingredients—dry and wet—are being combined in the bowl and the mixture stirred until all the flour is dampened. Then the batter is beaten vigorously for just 1 minute. Time your beating by the clock and make every stroke count, for a quick thorough beating is essential to the success of this cake.

☼

4 At the end of the baking period the golden brown, evenly risen layers are taken from the oven, placed immediately on a cake rack, and allowed to remain in the pans for about 5 minutes. The cake is then loosened from the sides with a spatula and turned onto the rack. Remove paper from bottom of cake (if one was used) and turn cake right side up to finish cooling.

Quickest, easiest way to mix butter cake

*When time is scarce
let this cake
come to your rescue*

1. Sifting all the dry ingredients combines them speedily

2. Mix beaten eggs, milk, vanilla; add soft butter to flour

3. Combine all the ingredients with vigorous beating

4. When baked, cool slightly on rack; remove from pans

Here is a cake mixed by the muffin method.
All the dry ingredients are sifted together, the liquids are combined
and added with the softened butter, and the batter beaten vigorously

SMALL CAKES

1⅔ cups sifted Swans Down Cake Flour
1½ teaspoons Calumet Baking Powder
⅓ cup butter or other shortening   1 cup sugar
2 eggs, well beaten   ½ cup milk   1 teaspoon flavoring

Sift flour once, measure, add baking powder, and sift together three times. Cream butter thoroughly, add sugar gradually, and cream together until light and fluffy. Add eggs, then flour, alternately with milk, a small amount at a time. Beat after each addition until smooth. Add flavoring. Pour into greased cup-cake pans, filling them ⅔ full. Bake in moderate oven (375° F.) 20 minutes, or until done. Cover with Orange Butter Frosting (page 107), Seven Minute Frosting (page 104), or Clever Judy Frosting (page 108). Decorate cakes simply in any way desired. Makes 2 dozen cup cakes. *Basic Recipe 8*

KEY STEPS

1 How to fill small pans
2 How to cut attractive small cakes from layers or sheets for novelties
3 How to frost tiny cakes
4 How to decorate little frosted cakes effectively

1 Just a word of caution about filling pans. For perfectly shaped cakes, do not fill pans more than ⅔ full. If too much batter is poured into the little cups, the cakes rise over the tops during the baking and the edges have to be trimmed.

☼

2 You may prefer to bake the batter in a square or oblong pan and cut it when cold into fancy shapes. If so, use a long sharp knife and cut cake into strips. Then cut strips into squares, diamonds, or other desired shapes. Cut with firm, sure strokes to avoid ragged edges. Fancy cutters may also be used.

☼

3 A butter frosting, delicately tinted, is one of the simplest and prettiest decorations for small cakes. Before starting to frost, brush off all crumbs. Spread frosting on smoothly with a knife, using as few strokes as possible. For the final touch, decorate top simply with bits of candied peel or ginger, thin slices of citron, angelica, or candied cherries, or tiny colored candies.

☼

4 Seven Minute Frosting (page 104) is a favorite decoration for cup cakes. For cup cakes *de luxe*, dress up frosted cakes with some of the simple decorations illustrated. Pile frosting generously on top of the little cakes, swirling it prettily, then sprinkle tops with snowy shreds of coconut, bits of chocolate, or coarsely chopped nuts. Or press half a cherry or nut into center lightly. White frosting may be tinted delicately to carry out any desired color scheme.

Some suggestions for making small cakes

*With these cake tricks
a clever hostess
plays a winning hand*

1. Fill small cake pans about two-thirds full of batter

2. Layer or sheet cake may be cut into fancy shapes

3. Spread butter frosting smoothly and decorate simply

4. Or top with swirls of fluffy frosting and decorate

Attractive little cakes made by baking butter cake batter in small pans, or in layer or sheet pans and then cutting into fancy shapes. Also some points about frosting and decorating

53

CALUMET QUICK CAKE

(2 egg whites)

2 cups sifted Swans Down Cake Flour   2 teaspoons Calumet Baking Powder
½ teaspoon salt   1 cup sugar   4 tablespoons softened butter or other shortening
2 egg whites, stiffly beaten   ½ cup milk
½ teaspoon vanilla

Sift flour once, measure, add baking powder, salt, and sugar, and sift together three times. Add butter and egg whites. Combine milk and vanilla
and add to flour mixture, stirring until all flour is dampened. Then beat
vigorously 1 minute. Bake in two greased 8-inch layer pans in moderate
oven (375° F.) 20 to 25 minutes. Spread Luscious Lemon Frosting (page
107) between layers and on top and sides of cake.

✿

CREOLE TIER CAKE

Use recipe for Calumet Quick Cake (above). Cool after baking. Cut layers
crosswise in halves. Spread Creole Butter Frosting (double recipe, page
109) between layers and on top of cake. Serve in wedges.

✿

ALADDIN CHOCOLATE CAKE

(2 eggs)

1⅓ cups sifted Swans Down Cake Flour   1¾ teaspoons Calumet Baking Powder
¼ teaspoon salt   1 cup sugar   5 tablespoons softened butter or other shortening
2 eggs, well beaten   ½ cup milk   ½ teaspoon vanilla
2 squares Baker's Unsweetened Chocolate, melted

Sift flour once, measure, add baking powder, salt, and sugar, and sift together three times. Add butter. Combine eggs, milk, and vanilla, and add
to flour mixture, stirring until all flour is dampened. Add chocolate and
blend. Then beat vigorously 1 minute. Bake in a greased pan, 8x8x2
inches, in moderate oven (325° F.) 1 hour. Spread Chocolate Butter Frosting (page 108) on top and sides of cake.

✿

QUICK SPICE CAKE

(2 eggs)

2 cups sifted Swans Down Cake Flour   2 teaspoons Calumet Baking Powder
¼ teaspoon salt   ½ teaspoon cinnamon   ½ teaspoon nutmeg
¼ teaspoon cloves   ¾ cup sugar
5 tablespoons softened butter or other shortening   ¼ cup molasses
2 eggs, well beaten   ½ cup milk

Sift flour once, measure, add baking powder, salt, spices, and sugar, and
sift together three times. Add butter and molasses. Combine eggs and milk
and add to flour mixture, stirring until all flour is dampened. Then beat
vigorously 1 minute. Bake in two greased 8-inch layer pans in moderate
oven (375° F.) 20 to 25 minutes. Spread Coffee Frosting (page 109) between
layers and on top and sides of cake.

WALNUT CREAM CAKES

1 recipe Toasted Walnut Filling
½ cup cream, whipped   12 large cup cakes

Combine filling and cream. Cut thin slice from top of each cup cake, hollow out center, and fill with cream mixture. Replace top. Frost, if desired.

Toasted Walnut Filling

¼ cup brown sugar, firmly packed   3 tablespoons butter   1 teaspoon water
1 egg yolk, slightly beaten
⅓ cup walnut meats, slightly broken and toasted

Combine sugar, butter, water, and egg yolk in top of double boiler. Place over rapidly boiling water and cook until mixture is slightly thickened, stirring constantly. Add nuts. Cool; use plain or with cream to fill cakes.

¤

GINGER TEA CAKES
(1 egg)

1½ cups sifted Swans Down Cake Flour   1½ teaspoons Calumet Baking Powder
¼ teaspoon soda   ½ teaspoon salt   ½ teaspoon cinnamon
¼ teaspoon cloves   1½ teaspoons ginger   ¼ cup butter or other shortening
4 tablespoons brown sugar   1 egg, well beaten
½ cup molasses   ½ cup boiling water

Sift flour once, measure, add baking powder, soda, salt, and spices, and sift together three times. Cream butter thoroughly, add sugar gradually, and cream together until light and fluffy. Add egg and beat well. Add flour, alternately with molasses, a small amount at a time, beating after each addition until smooth. Add boiling water, mixing quickly to blend. Turn into small greased cup-cake pans, filling them ½ full, and bake in moderate oven (375° F.) 20 minutes, or until done. Cool. Cover tops of cakes with Butter Frosting (page 107). To vary, make slit in cakes and insert slice of preserved ginger before frosting. Makes 2 dozen tea cakes.

¤

ORANGE TEA CAKES
(1 egg)

2 cups sifted Swans Down Cake Flour   2 teaspoons Calumet Baking Powder
¼ teaspoon salt   1 tablespoon grated orange rind
2 tablespoons butter or other shortening   1 cup sugar   1 egg, unbeaten
¼ cup milk   ½ cup orange juice

Sift flour once, measure, add baking powder and salt, and sift together three times. Add orange rind to butter and cream well. Add sugar gradually, and cream together thoroughly. Add egg and beat until light and fluffy. Add flour, alternately with milk and orange juice, a small amount at a time. Beat after each addition until smooth. Pour into greased cupcake pans, filling them ⅔ full. Bake in moderate oven (375° F.) 20 minutes, or until done. Cover with Orange Butter Frosting (½ recipe, page 107). Makes 12 large or 20 small cup cakes.

DATE SURPRISES

3 cups sifted flour
2 teaspoons Calumet Baking Powder
½ teaspoon salt   ⅔ cup butter or other shortening
½ cup brown sugar, firmly packed   1 egg, well beaten
1 teaspoon vanilla   ⅓ cup milk

Sift flour once, measure, add baking powder and salt, and sift again. Cream butter thoroughly, add sugar gradually, and cream together until light and fluffy. Add egg and vanilla; then flour, alternately with milk, a small amount at a time, beating until smooth. Chill thoroughly. Roll ⅛ inch thick. Cut with 2½-inch floured cutter. Place 1 teaspoon Date Filling (page 60) on a circle, place another circle on top, and press edges together. Bake on ungreased baking sheet in hot oven (400° F.) 10 to 12 minutes. Makes about 3 dozen. *Basic Recipe 9*

KEY STEPS

1 How to work in last of flour for a stiff dough

2 How to roll the dough

3 How to cut cooky circles

4 How to put the filling into the cookies and how to crimp the edges

1 Mix these cookies like butter cake, blending in last of flour with back of paddle or spoon. The dough should be soft, but not sticky . . . a trifle stiff, yet not hard. Now a brief chilling (15 minutes or more) in the refrigerator to permit handling the dough without the addition of more flour. If extra flour has to be added during the rolling, cookies are not as tender or delicious.

☼

2 Rolling out cookies is simple when your dough behaves properly. Work with half or less of the dough at a time, keeping remainder in refrigerator until ready to roll. Flour board and rolling pin *slightly* . . . use only enough flour to keep dough from sticking. Move dough about to prevent sticking. Roll ⅛ inch thick.

☼

3 In cutting out cookies, dip cutter in flour each time before using to keep dough from sticking. Cut cookies carefully, so that they will be perfect in shape, but cut them close together in order to get as many as possible from the first rolling. Cookies cut from dough that has been rolled more than once are never so tender.

☼

4 There's as much of a trick in putting the filling in these cookies and keeping it there, as there is in enclosing an apple in a dumpling. Spread filling evenly over cooky, keeping it away from edges. Then place another cooky on top and press edges together with tines of fork dipped in flour. The crimped edge is decorative and also helps to keep filling from trickling out during baking.

Best, easiest way to make rolled cookies

*To keep soft cookies moist,
crisp ones, dry—
store each type separately*

1. Chill cooky dough until firm
enough to roll

2. Roll dough from center out
with light, deft motion

3. Cut as many cookies as possible
from first rolling

4. The attractive crimped edge
helps seal in filling

A thorough chilling of the soft dough makes
easy to handle, and skillful cutting gives more and better shaped
cookies. Filled cookies are a popular version of cut-out cookies

57

VANILLA NUT COOKIES

4 cups sifted flour
3 teaspoons Calumet Baking Powder
¼ teaspoon salt   1 cup butter or other shortening
½ cup brown sugar, firmly packed
2 cups granulated sugar   2 eggs, well beaten
1 cup nut meats, chopped   1 tablespoon vanilla

Sift flour once, measure, add baking powder and salt, and sift again. Cream butter thoroughly, add sugars gradually, and cream together until light and fluffy. Add eggs, nuts, and vanilla. Add flour gradually, mixing well. Shape into rolls, 1½ inches in diameter, and roll in waxed paper. Chill overnight, or until firm enough to slice. Cut into ⅛-inch slices. Bake on ungreased baking sheet in a hot oven (425° F.) 5 minutes, or until done. Makes 7 dozen cookies.

Basic Recipe 10

KEY STEPS

1 How to blend all ingredients for smooth dough

2 How to shape dough into rolls or pack in mold

3 How to store rolls for chilling in refrigerator

4 How to slice the cookies

1 The sifted dry ingredients are beaten into the butter, sugar, and egg mixture about ¼ at a time. With the first additions the mixture is soft enough to blend easily and quickly. When mixture becomes stiff, the flour is worked in with the back of paddle or wooden spoon. Note that the nuts and vanilla are added before the flour in this stiff mixture to avoid any extra difficult mixing.

☼

2 This stiff dough is inclined to crumble. Gather together all loose particles and press lightly into one large piece of dough. It may then be divided in half and shaped into rolls, or packed into attractive molds for chilling.

☼

3 For rolls, work with half the dough at a time. Fold waxed paper over dough, press lightly, and mold into roll about 1½ inches in diameter, lengthening as you shape. Wrap paper tightly and pat outside of paper, making dough smooth and even. For molds, pack dough firmly into mold; avoid leaving any empty spaces or holes. Chill cooky dough as soon as shaped.

☼

4 Hold firm dough with left hand and, with a long, sharp, thin bladed knife, cut into thin slices. Use a sawing motion, drawing knife back and forth through dough, and, at the same time, pressing down lightly. Do not press too hard or allow dough to become softened if cookies are to be shapely.

Ice box cookies—a modern convenience

Slice and bake as needed
. . . in ten minutes
you'll have fresh cookies

1. Blend well after each addition of sifted flour mixture

2. Press dough together lightly in one large ball

3. Shaping dough into rolls or molds is fascinating

4. Chill shaped dough until firm before trying to slice

No rolling needed—no cooky cutters used. Just neat rolls of chilled, firm dough from which nicely formed cookies may be sliced and freshly baked whenever they are wanted

OLD-FASHIONED SUGAR COOKIES

2¼ cups sifted flour   1½ teaspoons Calumet Baking Powder
¼ teaspoon salt   ½ teaspoon nutmeg
1½ teaspoons grated lemon rind   ½ cup butter or other shortening
1 cup sugar   2 eggs, well beaten   1 tablespoon cream

Sift flour once, measure, add baking powder, salt, and nutmeg, and sift
again. Add lemon rind to butter and cream thoroughly. Add sugar gradually, and cream together until light and fluffy. Add eggs and cream; then
beat thoroughly. Add flour gradually and blend. Chill until firm enough
to roll. Roll ⅛ inch thick on slightly floured board. Cut with 3½-inch
floured cutter and sprinkle with sugar. Bake on ungreased baking sheet
in hot oven (400° F.) 10 minutes. Makes 3 dozen cookies.

✿

SAND TARTS

2 cups sifted Swans Down Cake Flour   1½ teaspoons Calumet Baking Powder
½ cup butter or other shortening   1 cup sugar   1 egg, well beaten
1 egg white, slightly beaten   1 tablespoon sugar   ¼ teaspoon cinnamon
1 cup blanched almonds, split

Sift flour once, measure, add baking powder, and sift again. Cream butter
thoroughly, add sugar gradually, and cream together until light and fluffy.
Add egg and flour. Blend. Chill until firm enough to roll. Roll ⅛ inch thick
on slightly floured board. Cut with floured doughnut cutter. Brush with
egg white and sprinkle with mixture of sugar and cinnamon. Arrange 3
halves of split almonds on each cooky. Bake on ungreased baking sheet in
moderate oven (375° F.) 10 minutes. Makes 6 dozen cookies.

✿

ROLLED BUTTERSCOTCH COOKIES

3 cups sifted flour   2¼ teaspoons Calumet Baking Powder
½ teaspoon salt   ¾ cup butter   1¼ cups brown sugar, firmly packed
2 eggs, unbeaten   1½ teaspoons vanilla   1½ teaspoons lemon juice

Sift flour once, measure, add baking powder and salt, and sift again. Cream
butter thoroughly, add sugar gradually, and cream together until light and
fluffy. Add eggs and beat well. Add vanilla and lemon juice; then add flour,
mixing well. Chill until firm enough to roll. Roll ⅛ inch thick on slightly
floured board. Cut with floured cutter and decorate, if desired. Bake on
ungreased baking sheet in hot oven (425° F.) 5 to 6 minutes. Makes 7
dozen cookies. For decorating, use nuts, citron, raisins, or dates.

✿

DATE FILLING FOR DATE SURPRISES

2 cups dates, seeded and chopped   ⅔ cup sugar
⅔ cup boiling water   1 tablespoon lemon juice   1 tablespoon butter

Cook dates, sugar, and water 6 to 8 minutes, or until thick, stirring constantly. Remove from fire; add lemon juice and butter. Cool.

PEANUT BUTTER ICE BOX COOKIES

2 cups sifted flour   3 teaspoons Calumet Baking Powder
½ teaspoon salt   1½ cups Post's Whole Bran   ½ cup butter or other shortening
½ cup peanut butter   ½ cup brown sugar, firmly packed
1½ cups granulated sugar   2 eggs, well beaten   3 tablespoons milk

Sift flour once, measure, add baking powder and salt, and sift again. Add Post's Whole Bran. Cream butter thoroughly, add peanut butter, and cream together until smooth. Add sugars gradually and cream well. Add eggs and blend. Add flour mixture, alternately with milk. Shape in a 1½-inch roll, wrap in waxed paper. Chill thoroughly. Cut in ¼-inch slices. Bake on greased sheet in hot oven (400° F.) 8 minutes. Makes 4 dozen.

✺

CHOCOLATE WALNUT DOLLARS

2¼ cups sifted flour   1½ teaspoons Calumet Baking Powder
½ teaspoon cinnamon   1 egg, slightly beaten   1 cup sugar
½ cup soft butter or other shortening   2 tablespoons milk
2 squares Baker's Unsweetened Chocolate, melted
½ cup walnut meats, chopped   1 teaspoon vanilla

Sift flour once, measure, add baking powder and cinnamon, and sift together three times. Combine remaining ingredients, then add flour, mixing well. Shape in 2-inch roll, wrap in waxed paper; chill thoroughly. Cut in ⅛-inch slices. Bake on ungreased sheet in hot oven (400° F.) 8 minutes. Makes 48.

✺

COCONUT ICE BOX COOKIES

2 cups sifted flour   1½ teaspoons Calumet Baking Powder
⅛ teaspoon salt   ½ cup butter or other shortening
1 cup granulated sugar   ¼ cup brown sugar, firmly packed   1 egg, well beaten
1 cup Baker's Coconut, Premium Shred   1½ teaspoons vanilla

Sift flour once, measure, add baking powder and salt; sift again. Cream butter, add sugars, then remaining ingredients. Add flour gradually. Shape in 1½-inch rolls; wrap in waxed paper. Chill thoroughly. Cut in ⅛-inch slices. Bake on ungreased sheet in hot oven (425° F.) 5 minutes. Makes 40.

✺

CHOCOLATE PIN WHEELS

1½ cups sifted flour   ½ teaspoon Calumet Baking Powder
⅛ teaspoon salt   ½ cup butter or other shortening   ½ cup sugar
1 egg yolk, well beaten   3 tablespoons milk
1 square Baker's Unsweetened Chocolate, melted

Sift flour once, measure, add baking powder and salt, and sift again. Cream butter thoroughly, add sugar gradually, and cream together well. Add egg yolk. Add flour, alternately with milk, beating after each addition until smooth. Divide dough in two parts. To one add chocolate. Chill. Roll each half into rectangular sheet, ⅛ inch thick. Place chocolate sheet on top. Roll as for jelly roll. Chill thoroughly. Cut in ⅛-inch slices. Bake on ungreased sheet in hot oven (400° F.) 5 minutes. Makes 3½ dozen.

The Sponge Cake Leaders
With Their Many Popular Relatives

THERE are four basic recipes for sponge cakes in this book. First of these is angel food cake, a queen among cakes, and one which is regarded by home bakers as a supreme test of skill. Then comes a traditional sponge cake, almost as glamorous. The third lesson introduces a popular, modern version of sponge cake in which baking powder does much of the leavening, very efficiently and very economically. Finally, you find a lesson on jelly roll which makes you wise enough—and brave enough—to attempt not only that coveted cake but also other rolled cakes, which you may not have known had anything to do with sponge cake technic.

Each basic recipe, with its three or four supporting recipes, represents a quite distinct type of product, suitable for different needs, particularly pleasing to different tastes. For certain special occasions, angel food cake, or some variation of it, seems exactly right; as an accompaniment to fruit or ice cream, sponge cake is famous. And rolled sponge cakes for desserts have a place all their own. As you can see by this chart, you'll have nineteen grand cakes at your command, when you have mastered these four sponge cake lessons.

BASIC RECIPE	DESCRIPTION	RECIPES SIMILAR TO BASIC RECIPE
11. Swans Down Angel Food (page 64)	The standard angel food— queen of cakes	Coconut Crested Angel Food Cherry Angel Food Chocolate Angel Food Daffodil Cake *(Recipes on page 68)*
12. Swans Down Sponge Cake (page 66)	The standard sponge cake—a cake of tradition	Little Sponge Cakes Ice Cream Shortcake Creole Sponge Cake Sunshine Cake *(Recipes on page 69)*
13. Hot Milk Sponge Cake (page 70)	An economical baking powder sponge cake	Sponge Squares with Berry Topping Orange Sponge Cake Orange Custard Sponge Cake Fruited Sponge Torte *(Recipes on page 74)*
14. Old-fashioned Jelly Roll (page 72)	A simple sheet sponge for perfect jelly roll	Lemon Sponge Roll Butterscotch Spice Roll Snow-whirl Chocolate Roll *(Recipes on page 75)*

Jelly roll, coconut angel food,
a chocolate roll, a sunshine cake, and daffodil cake
—every one of these belongs to the sponge cake clan

The versatile sponge cake clan

SWANS DOWN ANGEL FOOD

1 cup sifted Swans Down Cake Flour
1 cup (8 to 10) egg whites   ¼ teaspoon salt
1 teaspoon cream of tartar   1¼ cups sifted granulated sugar
¾ teaspoon vanilla   ¼ teaspoon almond extract

Sift flour once, measure and sift four more times. Beat egg whites and salt with flat wire whisk. When foamy, add cream of tartar, and continue beating until eggs are stiff enough to hold up in peaks, but not dry. Fold in sugar carefully, 2 tablespoons at a time, until all is used. Fold in flavoring. Then sift small amount of flour over mixture and fold in carefully; continue until all is used. Pour batter into ungreased angel food pan and bake in slow oven. Begin at 275° F. After 30 minutes increase heat slightly (325° F.); bake 30 minutes more. Remove from oven; invert pan 1 hour. *Basic Recipe 11*

KEY STEPS

1 How to sift flour well
2 How to beat egg whites and when to *stop* beating
3 How to fold sugar and flour into the egg whites
4 How to bake angel food and cool it after baking

---

1 The flour is sifted again and again. We like to sift ours five times —once just before measuring and then four times more. This repeated sifting incorporates more and more air, making the flour as light as so much thistledown. This airiness is important in securing an angel food that is feathery light. Note the convenience of sifting flour on two squares of paper.

✿

2 Beat 1 cup egg whites with flat wire whisk until foamy, then add cream of tartar. Continue to beat, using a gentle motion that keeps the wire whisk below the surface, until the egg whites are light and thick, but not dry. When whisk is lifted out, the whites pile up in moist, glossy peaks. The air bubbles are now very fine and even. These snowy, fluffy, slightly moist egg whites are essential.

✿

3 The sugar is sprinkled over the beaten egg whites, about 2 tablespoons at a time, then gently folded in by a cutting-down, lifting-up and folding-over motion. Then the flour is sifted gradually over the fluffy mixture and folded in with the same rhythmic technic. The folding continues only until ingredients are blended. Angel food batter is beautifully light and fluffy with a satiny white sheen.

✿

4 The pan in which angel food is baked is never greased. It is then possible for the batter to cling to sides of pan as it bakes and thus rise to its full height. Cutting down through batter with a spatula removes any large air bubbles. A long, slow baking and careful cooling transforms the fluffy batter into a master angel food.

Standard way of making angel food cake

*Gently tear—never cut
the rule for
the sponge cake family*

1. Squares of paper are handy for sifting the flour

2. Beat egg whites with whisk until stiff—not dry

3. Deft, light handling tells the mixing story

4. Cut through batter to remove large air bubbles

Into egg whites, beaten carefully to a moist, glossy stiffness, sugar is folded gradually. Lastly, flour is added by the same gentle down-up-and-over motion. The batter is baked slowly

SWANS DOWN SPONGE CAKE

1 cup sifted Swans Down Cake Flour
¼ teaspoon salt   Grated rind and juice of ½ lemon
5 egg yolks, beaten until thick and lemon-colored
5 egg whites   1 cup sifted sugar

Sift flour once, measure, add salt, and sift together four times.
Add lemon rind and juice to beaten egg yolks and beat with
rotary egg beater until very thick and light. Beat egg whites
with flat wire whisk until stiff enough to hold up in peaks, but
not dry. Fold in sugar, a small amount at a time; then egg yolks.
Fold in flour, a small amount at a time. Bake in ungreased tube
pan in slow oven (325° F.) 1 hour, or until done. Remove from
oven and invert pan 1 hour, or until cake is thoroughly cold,
before removing from pan. (See illustration and directions on
page 27 for removing cake from pan.) *Basic Recipe 12*

(See illustration and directions on page 27 for removing cake from pan.)

KEY STEPS

1 How to beat egg yolk
2 How to fold sugar int
   stiffly beaten egg white
3 How to blend egg yolks
   flour, and egg white mix
   ture to insure lightness
4 How to bake sponge cak

1 The egg yolks must be beaten long and vigorously to incorporate
all the air possible. Do not stop beating until yolks are thick and
a lemon yellow in color. Then add lemon rind and juice, and continue beating—this time until eggs are very thick and light in color
Lemon juice stiffens cell walls of the eggs and so helps to retain air

☼

2 The sugar is sprinkled over the stiffly beaten egg whites, about ?
tablespoons at a time; it is carefully mixed in by cutting down
into the whites with tablespoon, then lifting up and folding over
This technic becomes a deft, rolling motion. Next, the egg yolks are
folded in with the same careful down-up-and-over motion, thus
keeping all the air bubbles in the feathery light batter.

☼

3 As soon as the yellow streams of egg yolk have fused with the
egg white mixture, it is time to fold in the flour. Sprinkle it on
in small amounts—a little flour, a little folding, more flour, then
more folding, until all the flour has been carefully blended in without losing a bit of the spongy lightness of the batter.

☼

4 Bake this fluffy mixture in a tube pan that is ungreased, so that
the delicate structure of cake may cling to the sides of the pan
for support as it rises. Place it in a slow oven (325° F.) for a long
even baking; it takes about 1 hour. This low temperature insures
tenderness. Be sure that the cake is thoroughly baked before removing it from the oven.

Standard method of making sponge cake

*Moist, tender, airy-light
—and a cake
that you need not frost*

1. Add lemon juice to beaten yolks to beat thicker still

2. Fold sugar gradually into stiffly beaten egg whites

3. Sift flour over sponge mixture to safeguard lightness

4. Pour mixture into ungreased pan; bake carefully

Egg yolks, beaten thick and light, are blended with the mixture of beaten egg whites and sugar; flour is then folded in gradually, and the batter turned into an ungreased pan

COCONUT CRESTED ANGEL FOOD

Use recipe for Swans Down Angel Food (page 64). Pour batter into ungreased angel food pan. Sprinkle with ½ cup Baker's Coconut, Premium Shred. Bake in slow oven at least 1 hour. Begin at 275° F. and after 30 minutes increase heat slightly (325° F.) and bake 30 minutes longer.

☼

CHERRY ANGEL FOOD

Use recipe for Swans Down Angel Food (page 64). Pour about ⅓ of cake batter into ungreased angel food pan. Sprinkle ¼ cup finely chopped maraschino cherries over it, add another ⅓ of batter, then ¼ cup cherries, and remaining batter. Run knife through to bottom of pan to mix cherries evenly throughout. Bake in slow oven at least 1 hour. Begin at 275° F. and after 30 minutes increase heat slightly (325° F.) and bake 30 minutes.

☼

CHOCOLATE ANGEL FOOD
(10 to 12 egg whites)

¾ cup sifted Swans Down Cake Flour   4 tablespoons Baker's Breakfast Cocoa
1¼ cups egg whites   ¼ teaspoon salt   1 teaspoon cream of tartar
1¼ cups sifted granulated sugar   1 teaspoon vanilla

Sift flour once, measure, add cocoa, and sift four more times. Beat egg whites and salt with flat wire whisk. When foamy, add cream of tartar and continue beating until eggs are stiff enough to hold up in peaks, but not dry. Fold in sugar carefully, 2 tablespoons at a time, until all is used. Fold in vanilla. Then sift small amount of flour over mixture and fold in carefully; continue until all is used. Pour batter into ungreased angel food pan and bake in slow oven at least 1 hour. Begin at 275° F. and after 30 minutes increase heat slightly (325° F.) and bake 30 minutes longer. Remove from oven and invert pan 1 hour, or until cold.

☼

DAFFODIL CAKE
(8 to 10 egg whites and 4 egg yolks)

1 cup sifted Swans Down Cake Flour
1¼ cups sifted sugar   1 cup egg whites   ½ teaspoon salt
1 teaspoon cream of tartar   ½ teaspoon vanilla
½ teaspoon orange extract   4 egg yolks, beaten until thick and lemon-colored

Sift flour once, measure, add ¾ cup sugar, and sift four times. Beat egg whites and salt with flat wire whisk. When foamy, add cream of tartar; continue beating until stiff enough to hold up in peaks, but not dry. Beat in remaining sugar, 2 tablespoons at a time. Sift flour over mixture in small amounts, folding carefully. Divide in two parts. To one, fold in vanilla. To other, fold in orange extract and egg yolks. Put by tablespoons into ungreased angel food pan, alternating mixtures. Bake in slow oven (275° F.) and after 30 minutes increase heat slightly to 325° F. and bake 50 minutes longer. Remove from oven and invert pan 1 hour, or until cold.

68

LITTLE SPONGE CAKES

Use recipe for Swans Down Sponge Cake (page 66). Pour batter into small cup-cake pans which have been greased very lightly on bottoms. Bake in moderate oven (350° F.) 20 minutes, or until done. Remove carefully from pans. Makes 3 dozen little sponge cakes.

✿

ICE CREAM SHORTCAKE

Use recipe for Swans Down Sponge Cake (page 66). Cool after baking. Cut in 1½-inch wedges. Use two wedges of cake for each serving. Place a slice of brick ice cream on one and cover with the second, turning so that the narrow end of top cake wedge is above wide end of under cake wedge. Serve with sauce of crushed, sweetened berries or peaches. (Vanilla or fruit ice cream is suitable to use in this recipe.)

✿

CREOLE SPONGE CAKE

(5 eggs)

¾ cup sifted Swans Down Cake Flour   ¼ teaspoon salt
4 tablespoons Baker's Breakfast Cocoa   1 tablespoon lemon juice
5 egg yolks, beaten until thick and lemon-colored
5 egg whites   1 cup sifted sugar

Sift flour once, measure, add salt and cocoa, and sift together four times. Add lemon juice to beaten egg yolks and beat with rotary egg beater until very thick and light. Beat egg whites with flat wire whisk until stiff enough to hold up in peaks, but not dry. Fold in sugar, a small amount at a time; then egg yolks. Fold in flour, a small amount at a time. Bake in ungreased tube pan in slow oven (325° F.) 1 hour, or until done. Remove from oven and invert pan 1 hour, or until cold.

✿

SUNSHINE CAKE

(6 egg whites and 4 egg yolks)

1 cup sifted Swans Down Cake Flour   1 cup sifted sugar
¼ teaspoon salt   6 egg whites   ½ teaspoon cream of tartar
4 egg yolks, beaten until thick and lemon-colored   ½ teaspoon lemon extract

Sift flour once, measure, add ½ of sugar, and sift together four times. Add salt to egg whites and beat with flat wire whisk. When foamy, add cream of tartar, and continue beating until whisk leaves faint line when drawn across surface of egg whites. Add remaining sugar gradually, and continue beating as before, until texture is very fine and even and egg whites are stiff enough to hold up in peaks, but not dry. Fold in egg yolks and lemon extract. Then sift small amount of flour over mixture and fold in carefully; continue until all is used. Pour into ungreased tube pan and bake in slow oven (300° F.) 30 minutes, then increase heat slightly (325° F.) and bake 35 minutes longer. Remove from oven and invert pan 1 hour, or until cake is thoroughly cold, before removing from pan.

HOT MILK SPONGE CAKE

1 cup sifted Swans Down Cake Flour
1 teaspoon Calumet Baking Powder   3 eggs
1 cup sugar   2 teaspoons lemon juice   6 tablespoons hot milk

Sift flour once, measure, add baking powder, and sift together three times. Beat eggs until very thick and light and nearly white (10 minutes). Add sugar gradually, beating constantly. Add lemon juice. Fold in flour, a small amount at a time, until all is added. Add milk, mixing quickly until batter is smooth. Turn at once into ungreased tube pan and bake in moderate oven (350° F.) 35 minutes, or until done. Remove from oven and invert pan 1 hour, or until cold. Or bake in two lightly greased 8x8x2-inch pans in moderate oven (350° F.) 25 minutes. Sift powdered sugar over top. Cut in squares and serve as dessert or tea accompaniment.   *Basic Recipe 13*

KEY STEPS

1 Purpose of baking powder in this type of cake

2 How long to beat eggs

3 *Speedy* method of adding hot milk to mixture last

4 How to cool cake if baked in Swans Down pan

1   One level teaspoon Calumet Baking Powder is measured carefully and added to 1 cup sifted Swans Down Cake Flour. Then in three separate siftings these two ingredients are thoroughly mixed. Note that this sponge cake recipe calls for only 3 eggs—the baking powder furnishes the extra leavening needed.

☼

2   Thorough beating of eggs is one of the mixing secrets of this cake. With a sturdy rotary beater, beat eggs 10 minutes. Notice how thick and ivory colored they are! Then sprinkle sugar into the beaten eggs, beating constantly. After the last of the sugar has been thoroughly blended, add the lemon juice and then beat mixture to a fluffy, shining thickness.

☼

3   After folding sifted flour and baking powder into the mixture, add the hot milk all at once. Mix quickly and thoroughly until the batter is very smooth and light. The heat of the milk sets the bubbles of egg ever so slightly, giving them additional strength and thus helping to make a sponge cake of fluffy lightness.

☼

4   After the cake has baked 35 minutes, or longer in a moderate oven (350° F.), it is removed from the oven. The movable slides on pan are raised, the pan inverted, and cake allowed to cool in pan for about an hour. The movable slides are a special feature of the Swans Down angel food pan. They allow air to circulate and thus prevent the crust from steaming.

An economical way to make sponge cake

1. Add baking powder to flour and sift three times

2. Beat eggs 10 minutes; then beat in sugar gradually

3. Add hot milk all at once, mixing quickly and well

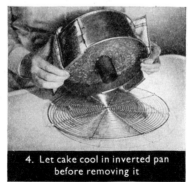

4. Let cake cool in inverted pan before removing it

Sponge cake of tender, fluffy lightness may be attained with fewer eggs if baking powder is used to furnish additional leavening. The four points illustrated are important

71

OLD-FASHIONED JELLY ROLL

¾ cup sifted Swans Down Cake Flour
¾ teaspoon Calumet Baking Powder
¼ teaspoon salt   4 eggs   ¾ cup sugar
1 teaspoon vanilla   1 cup jelly (any flavor)

Sift flour once; measure. Combine baking powder, salt, and eggs in bowl. Place over smaller bowl of hot water and beat with rotary egg beater, adding sugar gradually until mixture becomes thick and light-colored. Remove bowl from hot water. Fold in flour and vanilla. Turn into greased pan, 15x10 inches, lined with greased paper, and bake in hot oven (400° F.) 13 minutes. Quickly cut off crisp edges of cake. Turn from pan at once onto cloth covered with powdered sugar. Remove paper. Spread with jelly, spreading almost to edge. Roll quickly. Wrap in cloth and cool on rack.

Basic Recipe 14

KEY STEPS

1 Special way of beatin[g] eggs with baking powde[r]

2 How to prepare sheet pa[n] for baking sponge ro[ll]

3 How to cut crisp edge[s]

4 How to handle and ro[ll] sheet after it has bake[d]

1 Combine baking powder, salt, and eggs in a bowl set *over* not i[n] another, smaller bowl of hot water, with bottom of top bowl n[ot] quite touching the water. Beat with a rotary egg beater until firs[t] froth changes to a true foam. Then add sugar gradually, beatin[g] vigorously until a spongy, fluffy, golden mixture piles up in bow[l.] Remove bowl from over hot water. The flour is then gently folded i[n.]

☼

2 The batter is baked in a sheet pan, 15x10 inches. The pan first i[s] greased, then lined to within ½ inch of edge with waxed pape[r] and greased again—a triple protection that keeps bottom of cake sof[t] and smooth, makes it easy to remove and roll. The light, fluffy batte[r] is poured carefully into the pan and spread evenly with a spatul[a.]

☼

3 While cake is still in pan, cut off crisp edges quickly. Use a gen[-] tle sawing motion that does not tear the cake. Then invert pa[n] on a clean cloth which has been dusted with confectioners' suga[r] and coax the cake out with a spatula. Remove paper at once.

☼

4 Turn up edge of cake about 1 inch; lift up cloth high enough t[o] raise turned edge of cake off table. This starts cake rolling. Roll[-] ing continues as cloth is lifted higher and higher. Use left hand t[o] lift cloth and right hand to guide the rolling and keep cake straigh[t.] Stop when cake is entirely rolled and end of cake is underneath[.] Wrap cloth about cake tightly enough to keep rolled; cool on rack.

Jelly roll from a sheet of sponge cake

Before you cut and serve
a jelly roll
make sure that it is cool

1. Beat eggs and baking powder over hot water until thick

2. Bake in a specially prepared sheet pan with rim

3. Trim off crusts quickly before taking cake from pan

4. Roll cake while warm, letting it cool in cloth

Here is a method which calls for a unique mixing followed by a quick baking in a specially prepared pan. And after the cake is baked, a deft, swift technic to obtain a perfect roll

73

SPONGE SQUARES WITH BERRY TOPPING

Use the recipe for Hot Milk Sponge Cake (page 70). Bake in two lightly greased 8x8x2-inch pans, in moderate oven (350° F.) 25 minutes. Cut in squares and serve with Fresh Berry Topping.

Fresh Berry Topping

1 egg white   Dash of salt   ½ cup crushed berries
1½ cups sifted confectioners' sugar

Beat egg white and salt with rotary egg beater until frothy. Add berries, then add sugar gradually, beating until thick and fluffy.

✿

ORANGE SPONGE CAKE
(2 eggs and 1 egg yolk)

1¼ cups sifted Swans Down Cake Flour   1¼ teaspoons Calumet Baking Powder
¼ teaspoon salt   1 cup sugar   1 tablespoon grated orange rind
2 eggs and 1 egg yolk   ¼ cup orange juice   ¼ cup water

Sift flour once, measure, add baking powder and salt; sift together three times. Add ½ cup sugar and orange rind to eggs, and beat with rotary egg beater until thick and lemon-colored. Add remaining sugar gradually, beating thoroughly; then orange juice and water. Add flour gradually, beating with beater until smooth. Bake in ungreased tube pan, in moderate oven (350° F.) 55 minutes. Invert pan 1 hour, or until cold.

✿

ORANGE CUSTARD SPONGE CAKE

Prepare Orange Sponge Cake (above). When cool, split in halves. Spread with Custard Cream Filling. Sift powdered sugar over top. Serve in wedges.

Custard Cream Filling

3 tablespoons Swans Down Cake Flour   ⅓ cup sugar   Dash of salt
1 cup milk   1 egg yolk, slightly beaten   ½ teaspoon vanilla

Combine flour, sugar, and salt in top of double boiler; add milk and egg yolk. Place over rapidly boiling water and cook 10 minutes, or until thickened, stirring constantly. Cool; add flavoring.

✿

FRUITED SPONGE TORTE
(3 eggs)

1 cup sifted Swans Down Cake Flour   1 teaspoon Calumet Baking Powder
1 cup dates, seeded and coarsely cut   1 cup walnut meats, coarsely broken
1 cup sugar   1 teaspoon vanilla   3 egg yolks, well beaten
3 egg whites, stiffly beaten

Sift flour once, measure, add baking powder, and sift together three times. Add dates and nuts. Add sugar and vanilla to egg yolks, mixing thoroughly. Fold in flour mixture, then egg whites. Bake in two greased 9-inch layer pans in moderate oven (350° F.) ½ hour. Serve with whipped cream.

74

LEMON SPONGE ROLL

se recipe for Jelly Roll (page 72). Spread with Rich Lemon Filling.

Rich Lemon Filling

4 tablespoons Swans Down Cake Flour	¾ cup sugar	Dash of salt
¼ cup lemon juice	½ cup water	1 egg, well beaten
2 tablespoons butter	½ teaspoon grated lemon rind	

ombine flour, sugar, and salt in top of double boiler; add lemon juice,
ater, and egg. Place over rapidly boiling water, and cook 10 minutes, or
ntil thickened, stirring constantly. Add butter and lemon rind; cool.

☼

BUTTERSCOTCH SPICE ROLL
(4 eggs)

¾ cup sifted Swans Down Cake Flour		1 teaspoon cinnamon
¼ teaspoon cloves	¼ teaspoon allspice	¾ teaspoon Calumet Baking Powder
¼ teaspoon salt	4 eggs ¾ cup sifted sugar	1 teaspoon vanilla

ift flour once; measure, add spices, and sift together three times. Com-
ine baking powder, salt, and eggs in bowl. Place over smaller bowl of hot
vater and beat with rotary egg beater, adding sugar gradually until mix-
ure becomes thick and light-colored. Remove bowl from hot water. Fold
a vanilla and flour mixture. Turn into a greased pan, 15x10 inches, lined
vith greased paper, and bake in hot oven (400° F.) 13 minutes. Quickly
ut off crisp edges of cake. Turn from pan, remove paper, and cool slightly
n rack. Then spread with Butterscotch Cream Filling and roll.

Butterscotch Cream Filling

4 tablespoons Swans Down Cake Flour	⅓ cup brown sugar, firmly packed
⅛ teaspoon salt ⅔ cup water	2 tablespoons butter
1 teaspoon vanilla ¼ cup cream, whipped	

ombine flour, sugar, and salt in top of double boiler; add water. Place
ver rapidly boiling water and cook 10 minutes, or until thickened, stir-
ing constantly. Add butter. Cool and add vanilla and cream.

☼

SNOW-WHIRL CHOCOLATE ROLL
(4 eggs)

6 tablespoons sifted Swans Down Cake Flour	
6 tablespoons Baker's Breakfast Cocoa	½ teaspoon Calumet Baking Powder
¼ teaspoon salt ¾ cup sifted sugar	4 egg whites, stiffly beaten
4 egg yolks, beaten until thick and lemon-colored	1 teaspoon vanilla

ift flour once, measure, add cocoa, baking powder, and salt, and sift to-
ether three times. Fold sugar gradually into egg whites. Fold in egg yolks
nd vanilla. Fold in flour gradually. Pour into a greased pan, 15x10 inches,
ined with greased paper, and bake in hot oven (400° F.) 13 minutes.
Quickly cut off crisp edges of cake. Turn from pan at once onto cloth cov-
red with powdered sugar. Remove paper. Spread Seven Minute Frosting
(page 104) over cake and roll. Wrap in cloth until cool. Frost, if desired.

Quick Breads and Pastries
Branch from These Basic Types

✿

THE six lessons on quick breads and two on pastries charted below cover a large territory; yet cover it carefully and thoroughly. Each basic recipe highlights the secrets of success of a certain type of mixture, and makes easy and sure other recipes similar in method. When you have mastered the key recipes, you will feel competent to try all forty-six recipes named on this chart—treats for every meal.

BASIC RECIPE	DESCRIPTION	RECIPES SIMILAR TO BASIC RECIPE
15. Emergency Biscuits (page 78)	Drop biscuits— easiest and quickest of all	Cheese Drop Biscuits Fruit Drop Biscuits Pecan Drop Biscuits Cinnamon Drop Biscuits *(Recipes on page 82)*
16. Baking Powder Biscuits (page 80)	The standard baking powder biscuit	Cheese Roulettes Strawberry Shortcakes Quick Cinnamon Rolls *(Recipes on page 83)*
17. Quick Coffee Cake (page 84)	A novel sweet bread made with baking powder	Spiced Coffee Cake Swedish Tea Rolls Currant Coffee Rolls *(Recipes on page 88)*
18. Fruit Bread (page 86)	A standard baking powder bread	Calumet Nut Bread Calumet Raisin Bread Whole Bran Brown Bread Chocolate Bread Johnny Cake *(Recipes on page 89)*
19. Muffins (page 90)	The standard, simple muffin	Currant, Date, Apricot, Nut, Surprise, Spiced, Corn, and Bran Muffins *(Recipes on page 94)*
20. Griddle Cakes (page 92)	Griddle cakes— mixed easily and speedily	Sour Milk Griddle Cakes Waffles Toasted Coconut Waffles Bacon Waffles Cheese Waffles Jelly Pancakes *(Recipes on page 95)*
21. Pie Crust (page 96)	A sure way to flaky, tender pastry	Pie Shell Tart Shells Lemon Meringue Pie Vanity Fair Coconut Custard Pie Banana Pie Suprême *(Recipes on page 100)*
22. Cherry Pie (page 98)	A two-crust fruit pie with the juice sealed in	Calumet Pie Crust Two-crust Pie Fruit Pies Crisscross Apricot Pie *(Recipes on page 101)*

Here are favorites, old and new.
At the upper right are muffins; to the left, ears of corn.
Then come biscuits, some gems, and cheese roulettes

A new alphabet for quick breads

EMERGENCY BISCUITS

2 cups sifted flour
2 teaspoons Calumet Baking Powder   **½ teaspoon salt**
4 tablespoons butter or other shortening   **1 cup milk (about)**

Sift flour once, measure, add baking powder and salt, and sift again. Cut in shortening; add milk gradually, stirring until soft dough is formed. Drop from teaspoon on ungreased baking sheet. Bake in hot oven (450° F.) 12 to 15 minutes. Makes 12 biscuits. Here an approximate amount of liquid is given because flours vary slightly in the amount they absorb—due to gluten content or milling. Usually 1 cup minus 1 tablespoon milk is the amount needed for this soft dough. Swans Down Cake Flour makes especially light, tender biscuits and is so uniform that an exact proportion of liquid may always be used—¾ cup milk in this recipe.

Basic Recipe 15

KEY STEPS

1 How and why to sift the dry ingredients together

2 How to cut in the shortening for tender biscuit

3 How to mix the wet and dry ingredients quickly

4 How to "drop" biscuit

1 Measure 1 level teaspoon Calumet Baking Powder for each cup of sifted flour. Then into the sifter with the baking powder, flour and salt—all the dry ingredients together. One sifting does the job—distributing the leavening evenly in a moment's time.

☼

2 Cut shortening into flour quickly and lightly, being careful not to press down and mash the fat. The cutting is continued until the shortening is separated into tiny particles and the mixture resembles coarse corn meal. The pastry blender shown is a convenient little tool for cutting in shortening. Two knives may be used instead.

☼

3 Make a well in center of dry ingredients. Add about ½ of the liquid and start mixing immediately. Stir carefully at first to avoid splashing. Then mix vigorously, and add remaining liquid in small amounts until mixture forms a soft, sticky dough that clings to the sides of the bowl. This is an important step in making good biscuits; they must neither be overmixed nor undermixed.

☼

4 No kneading, no rolling, no shaping of dough. Just drop the dough from a teaspoon on a baking sheet. The soft mounds of dough will spread a little as they bake, so do not place them too close together if you want biscuits that are crusty all around. The biscuits should be baked in a hot oven (450° F.) for 12 to 15 minutes, or until risen and nicely browned.

The easiest and quickest biscuit method

hether dropped or rolled
all biscuits
should bake in a hot oven

1. Accurate measuring of baking powder is important

2. Cut in shortening until mixture resembles coarse meal

3. Add half of liquid to flour, mix; add remainder gradually

4. For "shaping" biscuits quickly, drop on baking sheet

Mixed and in the oven in a twinkling. Here are aking powder biscuits in the quickest, easiest style. No kneading, no rolling, no patting of the dough, no biscuit cutter needed

79

BAKING POWDER BISCUITS

2 cups sifted flour
2 teaspoons Calumet Baking Powder   ½ teaspoon salt
4 tablespoons butter or other shortening   ¾ cup milk (about)

Sift flour once, measure, add baking powder and salt, and sift again. Cut in shortening. Add milk gradually, stirring until soft dough is formed. Turn out on slightly floured board and knead 30 seconds, or enough to shape. Roll ½ inch thick and cut with 2-inch floured biscuit cutter. Bake on ungreased baking sheet in hot oven (450° F.) 12 to 15 minutes. Makes 12 biscuits. If slightly smaller biscuits are desired, cut with 1¾-inch cutter. Will make 16 biscuits. For tall biscuits, cut with 1¾-inch cutter and place biscuits close together in an 8x8x2-inch pan. To make very small tea biscuits, cut with 1½-inch cutter. Will make 24 biscuits.

Basic Recipe 16

KEY STEPS

1 How to add liquid—a then mix dough quick

2 How to knead the dou to make biscuits fla

3 How to pat or roll dough and cut biscu

4 How to bake the biscu

1 Pour about ½ of liquid into a little well made in sifted dry i gredients. Stir carefully at first, then vigorously, adding remai ing liquid gradually until mixture thickens enough to follow spo around bowl. This dough should be light and soft but not sticky.

☼

2 A brief kneading mixes ingredients quickly and develops fir flaky texture. Have your molding board—and hands—ever lightly dusted with flour. Knead mostly with right hand, guidi dough with the left. With finger tips, fold dough over, tucking it lightly, then lift fingers and press down quickly with ball of har pushing backward. Turn dough slightly; repeat. Knead 30 seconds.

☼

3 Pat dough lightly to ½-inch thickness with rolling pin dust with flour. Keep dough light and springy, being careful not press down heavily. Pat dough to an even thickness so that biscui will be uniform. If dough is rolled, rather than patted, push p lightly with a little lift at end of each roll.

☼

4 In cutting out biscuits, dip biscuit cutter lightly in flour ea time to prevent dough from sticking. Slip floured spatula gent under biscuit, pressing down against board, then lift biscuit car fully and place on ungreased baking sheet or in a shallow pan. this way the biscuits may be moved from the board to pan witho losing their shape. Place biscuits about an inch apart in pan if yo wish them to bake with an even brown crust all around.

Best method for baking powder biscui

Golden crust, tender crumb
light and flaky
behold these perfect biscuits

1. Mix carefully and quickly to form light, soft dough

2. Knead lightly for just 30 seconds to mix thoroughly

3. Pat dough into shape lightly with floured rolling pin

4. Place biscuits 1 inch apart on ungreased sheet

This method stresses quick, thorough mixing of ingredients, and light, brief kneading as essential to tender, flaky biscuits. From this dough many a delicious quick bread can be made

81

CHEESE DROP BISCUITS

2 cups sifted flour	2 teaspoons Calumet Baking Powder
½ teaspoon salt	1 cup grated American cheese
4 tablespoons butter or other shortening	1 cup milk (about)

Sift flour once, measure, add baking powder and salt, and sift again. Cut in cheese and shortening. Add milk gradually, stirring until soft dough is formed. Drop from teaspoon on ungreased baking sheet. Bake in hot oven (450° F.) 12 to 15 minutes. Makes 18. These biscuits are especially suitable to serve with fruit and vegetable salads for luncheon or supper menus.

✿

FRUIT DROP BISCUITS

2 cups sifted flour   2½ teaspoons Calumet Baking Powder
2 tablespoons sugar   ½ teaspoon salt   4 tablespoons butter or other shortening
¾ cup milk (about)   1 cup apple, pared, cored, and finely chopped
1½ teaspoons grated orange rind   ½ cup raisins, finely chopped

Sift flour once, measure, add baking powder, sugar, and salt, and sift again. Cut in shortening. Add milk gradually, stirring until soft dough is formed. Drop from teaspoon on ungreased baking sheet. Bake in hot oven (450° F.) 12 minutes. Makes 18. Serve for luncheon or tea.

✿

PECAN DROP BISCUITS

2 cups sifted Swans Down Cake Flour   2 teaspoons Calumet Baking Powder
3 tablespoons sugar   ½ teaspoon salt   4 tablespoons butter or other shortening
½ cup milk   1 egg, well beaten   ½ cup pecan meats, finely cut
1 tablespoon sugar   ⅛ teaspoon cinnamon

Sift flour once, measure, add baking powder, sugar, and salt, and sift again. Cut in shortening. Combine milk and egg, then add all at once to flour mixture and stir carefully until all flour is dampened. Add nuts and stir vigorously until mixture forms a soft dough that clings to sides of bowl. Drop from teaspoon on ungreased baking sheet. Sprinkle with mixture of sugar and cinnamon. Bake in hot oven (425° F.) 12 minutes. Makes 2½ dozen. These biscuits are dainty for tea.

✿

CINNAMON DROP BISCUITS

2 cups sifted Swans Down Cake Flour
2 teaspoons Calumet Baking Powder   3 tablespoons sugar
½ teaspoon salt   1 teaspoon cinnamon
4 tablespoons butter or other shortening   ½ cup milk   1 egg, well beaten

Sift flour once, measure, add baking powder, sugar, salt, and cinnamon, and sift again. Cut in shortening. Combine milk and egg, then add all at once to flour mixture and stir carefully until all flour is dampened. Then stir vigorously until mixture forms a soft dough that clings to sides of bowl. Drop from teaspoon on ungreased baking sheet. Sprinkle with additional sugar. Bake in hot oven (425° F.) 10 to 12 minutes. Makes 2½ dozen.

CHEESE ROULETTES

2 cups sifted flour   2 teaspoons Calumet Baking Powder
½ teaspoon salt   5 tablespoons butter or other shortening   ¾ cup milk (about)
Melted butter   1 cup grated American cheese   Salt   Paprika

Sift flour once, measure, add baking powder and salt, and sift again. Cut in shortening; add milk gradually, stirring until soft dough is formed. Turn out on slightly floured board and knead 30 seconds, or enough to shape. Roll into oblong sheet, ⅛ inch thick. Brush with melted butter. Spread cheese evenly over dough. Sprinkle with salt and paprika. Cut into strips, 6x½ inches, roll each strip, and place in greased muffin pans. Or roll sheet as for jelly roll, cut in ¾-inch slices, and place on greased baking sheet. Bake in hot oven (425° F.) 15 to 20 minutes. Makes 24.

✿

INDIVIDUAL STRAWBERRY SHORTCAKES

3 cups sifted Swans Down Cake Flour   3 teaspoons Calumet Baking Powder
1 teaspoon salt   ½ cup butter or other shortening   ¾ cup milk
2 quarts strawberries, crushed and sweetened

Sift flour once, measure, add baking powder and salt, and sift again. Cut in shortening; add milk all at once and stir carefully until all flour is dampened. Then stir vigorously until mixture forms a soft dough and follows spoon around bowl. Turn out immediately on slightly floured board and knead 30 seconds. Roll ¼ inch thick and cut with 3-inch floured biscuit cutter. Place half of circles on ungreased baking sheet; brush with melted butter. Place remaining circles on top and butter tops well. Bake in hot oven (450° F.) 15 to 20 minutes. Separate halves of hot biscuits, spread bottom halves with soft butter and some of strawberries. Place other halves on top. Spread with butter and remaining berries. Serves 8. Fresh raspberries, blackberries, cherries, sliced peaches, or apricots may also be used.

✿

QUICK CINNAMON ROLLS

2½ cups sifted Swans Down Cake Flour   2½ teaspoons Calumet Baking Powder
½ teaspoon salt   3 tablespoons butter or other shortening   ¾ cup milk
2 tablespoons butter   ⅓ cup brown sugar, firmly packed
½ teaspoon cinnamon   ½ cup currants or raisins
4 tablespoons butter   4 tablespoons brown sugar

Sift flour once, measure, add baking powder and salt, and sift again. Cut in shortening. Add milk all at once and stir carefully until all flour is dampened. Then stir vigorously until mixture forms a soft dough and follows spoon around bowl. Turn out immediately on slightly floured board and knead 30 seconds. Roll ¼ inch thick. Cream together butter, sugar, and cinnamon; spread on dough and sprinkle with currants. Roll as for jelly roll. Cut in 1¼-inch slices. Melt 4 tablespoons butter in 8x8x2-inch pan, add 4 tablespoons brown sugar, and mix well. Place rolls in pan, cut-side down. Bake in hot oven (425° F.) 15 minutes; reduce heat to moderate (350° F.) and bake 15 to 20 minutes longer. Remove from pan. Makes 12.

QUICK COFFEE CAKE

2 cups sifted flour
2 teaspoons Calumet Baking Powder   ¾ teaspoon salt
½ cup sugar   6 tablespoons butter or other shortening
1 egg, well beaten   ½ cup milk

1½ tablespoons melted butter   4 tablespoons sugar
1 tablespoon flour   ½ teaspoon cinnamon

Sift flour once, measure, add baking powder, salt, and sugar, and sift again. Cut in shortening. Combine egg and milk; add to flour mixture, stirring until mixture is blended. Turn into greased 9-inch layer pan, spreading dough evenly. Brush top with melted butter. Mix together sugar, flour, and cinnamon for topping and sift mixture evenly over dough. Bake in hot oven (400° F.) 25 to 30 minutes. Cut in wedges while in pan and remove pieces separately.

Basic Recipe 17

KEY STEPS

1 How to mix shorteni
and sifted flour mixtu

2 How to combine wet a
dry ingredients eas

3 How to spread dough o
in pan to make top ev

4 How to "top" the dou

1 Flour, baking powder, salt, sugar . . . these four, no more, all through the sifter together, directly into the mixing bowl. The the shortening joins them and is quickly cut in with a pastry blend er, or two knives, until the mixture has about the same appearan as that of rather coarse corn meal.

✿

2 The liquids are combined—the milk with the foamy, light, wel beaten egg. Then into the flour mixture they go—all at once. St gently and warily at first, to avoid splashing, then continue the mix ing with vigorous, energetic strokes until the two mixtures are we blended and the dough is smooth.

✿

3 The dough then goes into a greased 9-inch layer pan. It ma need a bit of coaxing with the spatula to spread it smoothly i the pan and draw it gently to the edge. But the top should be even s that the cake may rise evenly and be of uniform thickness.

✿

4 For a spicy topping, mix sugar, flour, and cinnamon togethe and sprinkle evenly over the buttered surface of the dough. small sifter is convenient for this purpose. Or, if using a spoon, tap gently, letting the mixture fall lightly. The topping has a more uni form color and a better flavor when the sugar and cinnamon ar blended before sprinkling on the dough.

Quick way to make delicious coffee cake

If you'll cut coffee cake in the pan topping will crumble less

1. All dry ingredients go through the sifter together

2. After addition of liquids, stir gently—then vigorously

3. Spread dough evenly in greased pan, using spatula

4. Sprinkle buttered dough with sugar and spice mixture

Baking powder—not yeast—is used to leaven this light, fluffy, up-to-date coffee cake. Dry ingredients are sifted together; liquid ingredients combined; then all are swiftly blended

85

FRUIT BREAD

2 cups sifted flour	4 teaspoons Calumet Baking Powder
1½ teaspoons salt	¾ cup sugar 2 cups Graham flour

¾ cup candied orange peel, thinly sliced

¾ cup nut meats, broken   2 eggs, well beaten

1⅔ cups milk   4 tablespoons melted butter or other shortening

Sift flour once, measure, add baking powder, salt, and sugar, and sift again. Combine Graham flour, orange peel, and nuts and add to flour mixture. Combine eggs, milk, and shortening. Add to flour and blend. Bake in two greased loaf pans, 7x3x2½ inches, in a moderate oven (350° F.) 1 hour, or until done. Remove from pans and cool thoroughly. Store overnight before slicing, for bread cannot be cut in thin, even slices when it is too fresh. For delicious sandwiches, cut in thin slices and spread with butter or cream cheese.   *Basic Recipe 18*

KEY STEPS

1 How to prepare nuts and fruit peel for loaves

2 How to combine dry ingredients, nuts, and peel

3 How to combine wet and dry ingredients correctly

4 How to bake fruit bread

1 Break walnut meats into rather small pieces and cut candied orange peel in thin slices before adding them to Graham flour Care in the preparation of these ingredients may make the difference between a loaf that slices easily and one which tears and pulls in slicing because it contains pieces of nuts and fruit that are too large.

☼

2 Combine sifted white flour, baking powder, sugar, and salt with mixture of Graham flour, nuts, and candied orange peel. (It is not necessary to sift coarse flours.) During the mixing, the nuts and peel are separated and coated with flour. This helps to keep them evenly distributed through the loaf during the baking, and prevents their sinking to the bottom in a layer.

☼

3 Use a bowl of the right size for beating the eggs. Beat the eggs to a foamy, fluffy lightness with a rotary egg beater. Pour in the milk and butter. Mix well. Add the combined liquids to the dry ingredients slowly—slowly—stirring briskly to prevent lumping. Then stir the mixture vigorously, but only enough to blend the ingredients

☼

4 Now into the oven—the batter evenly spread in two greased loaf pans, 7x3x2½ inches. A long, slow baking in a moderate oven (350° F.) lets the bread rise evenly and bake uniformly with a rich brown crust. After about 1 hour, the baking is finished, and the fragrant loaves are ready to come from the oven. They must be cooled and stored overnight, before slicing.

A delicious, quick baking powder bread

*When stored for a day
this fruit bread
cuts in thin, trim slices*

1. Break nut meats and cut candied peel in thin slices

2. Combine Graham flour mixture with white flour mixture

3. Add liquids slowly to flour mixture, stirring briskly

4. Remove from pans, cool; store overnight before slicing

Here is the proper technic for making bread leavened by baking powder. Special attention is given to the handling of coarse flours, fruits, and nuts, and to the baking of the bread

SPICED COFFEE CAKE

2 cups sifted flour   2 teaspoons Calumet Baking Powder
¾ teaspoon salt   ½ cup sugar   1 teaspoon cinnamon
¼ teaspoon mace   6 tablespoons butter or other shortening   1 egg, well beaten
½ cup milk   ½ cup currants

1½ tablespoons melted butter   4 tablespoons sugar   1 tablespoon flour
½ teaspoon cinnamon

Sift flour once, measure, add baking powder, salt, sugar, and spices, and sift again. Cut in shortening. Combine egg and milk; add to flour mixture, stirring carefully at first; then add currants and stir until mixture is blended. Turn into greased 9-inch layer pan, spreading dough evenly. Brush top with melted butter. Mix together sugar, flour, and cinnamon for topping and sift mixture evenly over dough. Bake in hot oven (400° F.) 25 to 30 minutes. Cut in wedges while in pan and remove pieces separately.

✿

SWEDISH TEA ROLLS

2 cups sifted Swans Down Cake Flour   2 teaspoons Calumet Baking Powder
½ teaspoon salt   ½ cup butter or other shortening   ⅔ cup milk

⅓ cup sugar   1 teaspoon cinnamon

Sift flour once, measure, add baking powder and salt, and sift again. Cut in shortening; add milk all at once and stir carefully until all flour is dampened. Then stir vigorously until mixture forms a soft dough and follows spoon around bowl. Turn out immediately on slightly floured board and knead 30 seconds. Roll ¼ inch thick. Cut in 2½-inch squares. Fold each square in half and press cut edges into mixture of sugar and cinnamon. Sprinkle thickly with more sugar and cinnamon. Place on ungreased baking sheet and bake in hot oven (450° F.) 15 minutes. Makes 15 to 18 rolls.

✿

CURRANT COFFEE ROLLS

3 cups sifted Swans Down Cake Flour   3 teaspoons Calumet Baking Powder
1 teaspoon salt   2 tablespoons sugar
½ cup butter or other shortening   ¾ cup milk

Melted butter   Sugar   ½ cup currants or seedless raisins
1 egg yolk, slightly beaten   4 tablespoons nut meats, finely chopped

Sift flour once, measure, add baking powder, salt, and sugar, and sift again. Cut in shortening; add milk all at once and stir carefully until all flour is dampened. Then stir vigorously until mixture forms a soft dough and follows spoon around bowl. Turn out immediately on slightly floured board and knead 30 seconds. Roll ⅛ inch thick and cut in 2½-inch squares. Brush with melted butter and sprinkle with sugar. Sprinkle currants over dough. Roll each square as for jelly roll. Brush with mixture of egg yolk and 1 tablespoon sugar, sprinkle generously with nuts. Place rolls on ungreased baking sheet and bake in hot oven (425° F.) 15 minutes, or until done. Makes 2½ dozen rolls.

CALUMET NUT BREAD

3 cups sifted flour   3 teaspoons Calumet Baking Powder   1 teaspoon salt
1 cup nut meats, chopped   3 tablespoons butter or other shortening
1 cup sugar   1 egg, well beaten   1¼ cups milk

Sift flour once, measure, add baking powder and salt, and sift together three times. Add nuts. Cream shortening, add sugar; then add egg, milk, and flour. Mix only until smooth. Bake in a greased loaf pan, 8x4x3 inches, in moderate oven (350° F.) 1 hour and 10 minutes.

Calumet Raisin Bread. Use raisins for nuts in recipe above.

✿

WHOLE BRAN BROWN BREAD

1½ cups sifted flour   3 teaspoons Calumet Baking Powder   ½ cup sugar
½ teaspoon salt   ½ cup raisins   1 cup milk
3 tablespoons molasses   1½ cups Post's Whole Bran   1 egg, well beaten
4 tablespoons melted butter or other shortening

Sift flour once, measure, add baking powder, sugar, and salt, and sift again. Add raisins. Pour milk and molasses over Post's Whole Bran; add egg and shortening. Add to flour mixture and blend. Bake in greased loaf pan, 8x4x3 inches, in moderate oven (350° F.) 1 hour, or until done.

✿

CHOCOLATE BREAD

3 cups sifted Swans Down Cake Flour   3 teaspoons Calumet Baking Powder
1¼ teaspoons salt   1 cup brown sugar, firmly packed   1 egg, well beaten
4 tablespoons melted butter or other shortening · 1¼ cups milk
2 squares Baker's Unsweetened Chocolate, melted

Sift flour once, measure, add baking powder and salt, and sift again. Add brown sugar and mix well. Add egg and shortening; then add milk gradually, mixing thoroughly. Add chocolate and blend. Bake in greased loaf pan, 8x4x3 inches, in moderate oven (350° F.) 1 hour and 15 minutes, or until done. When thoroughly cold, slice for tea sandwiches, spread with butter, with cream cheese and finely chopped walnuts, or with cream cheese and orange marmalade, and cut in narrow strips.

✿

JOHNNY CAKE
(Sour milk)

1¼ cups sifted flour   2 teaspoons Calumet Baking Powder   1 teaspoon salt
¾ teaspoon soda   2 tablespoons sugar   1 cup yellow corn meal
2 eggs, well beaten   1¼ cups sour milk or buttermilk
3 tablespoons melted shortening

Sift flour once, measure, add baking powder, salt, soda, and sugar, and sift again. Add corn meal. Combine eggs, milk and shortening. Add to dry ingredients, mixing well. Bake in a greased pan, 8x8x2 inches, in hot oven (425° F.) 40 minutes, or until done.

MUFFINS

2 cups sifted flour
2 teaspoons Calumet Baking Powder   2 tablespoons sugar
½ teaspoon salt   1 egg, well beaten   1 cup milk
4 tablespoons melted butter or other shortening

Sift flour once, measure, add baking powder, sugar, and salt and sift again. Combine egg, milk, and shortening. Add to flour, beating only enough to dampen all flour. Do not attempt to beat the mixture until smooth, but as soon as all flour is moistened, turn into greased muffin pans. Bake in hot oven (425° F.) 25 minutes, or until done. Makes 12 muffins. Muffin pans of different materials are suitable. Cast iron pans give an unusually even crust. They should first be heated and greased so the baking of the muffin mixture may not be retarded by the slow heating of the iron pans.   *Basic Recipe 19*

KEY STEPS

1 How to sift ingredients
2 How to combine liquids
3 How to combine the wet and dry ingredients — and when to stop mixing
4 How to grease muffin pans and fill with batter

1 For muffins of special lightness and fluffy tenderness, use Swans Down Cake Flour. All measurements should be accurate to obtain correct proportion of ingredients necessary for perfect muffins. Sift dry ingredients—flour, baking powder, sugar, and salt—together once. Sifting mixes these ingredients quickly and thoroughly. (With Swans Down Cake Flour, use ¾ cup milk in this recipe.)

☼

2 All liquid ingredients are mixed together. Beat egg until light and foamy and add milk. Melt butter slowly, preferably over hot water. Let butter cool slightly before adding to the egg and milk mixture to prevent it from hardening in small lumps.

☼

3 Turn wet ingredients all at once into dry ones. Stir as briskly as possible without splashing mixture out of mixing bowl. Stop stirring in about 25 seconds, or just as soon as all flour is *moistened.* The batter should look lumpy—do not attempt to beat it smooth. Overstirring results in muffins with sharp peaks or knobs on the outside and long holes or tunnels inside.

☼

4 Lift batter out lightly by spoonfuls into greased muffin pans filling them about ⅔ full. Have pans well greased so that the muffins will slip out easily. Partially fill any empty sections with water to avoid burning pan. Muffin pans of different materials may be used, such as cast iron, aluminum, glass, or tin. The pans may be small, medium, or large, according to size of muffin desired.

The standard method of making muffins

ruit muffins, nut muffins,
a jelly muffin
re made from this recipe

1. Sift flour, baking powder, sugar, and salt together once

2. Combine all liquids—beaten egg, milk, and melted butter

3. Stir only until all flour is dampened—avoid overmixing

4. No more stirring—quickly fill pans with spongy batter

Perfect muffins should be golden brown, light and fluffy, tender in crumb and fine in texture, and with no large holes or tunnels. To make them, just follow the steps pictured above

GRIDDLE CAKES

1 cup sifted flour
1 teaspoon Calumet Baking Powder
½ teaspoon salt   1 tablespoon sugar   1 egg, well beaten
¾ cup milk
3 tablespoons melted butter or other shortening

Sift flour once, measure, add baking powder, salt, and sugar, and sift again. Combine egg and milk. Add to flour gradually, beating to a smooth batter. Add shortening. Drop griddle cake batter from tip of tablespoon on hot, greased griddle. Bake, turning each cake when it is browned on underside and puffed and slightly set on top. Serve at once on warm plates with butter and Log Cabin Syrup. Makes 12 to 15 griddle cakes. For variety, serve these griddle cakes with marmalade, maple or brown sugar, or honey. *Basic Recipe 20*

KEY STEPS

1 How to beat the batter to make it very smooth

2 How to heat the griddle and test for readiness

3 How to drop the batter

4 When and how to turn cakes most successfully

1 The beaten egg and milk are combined, and added to the sifted flour mixture; these are quickly blended. The melted shortening is added last. A few turns of the rotary egg beater will make the batter satin-smooth. And, when Calumet Baking Powder is used there's no worry about beating out the leavening gas. Calumet's famous reserve action waits—to be released by heat.

☼

2 Heat the griddle slowly and evenly, being careful that it does not get too hot. To test the temperature of the griddle, place a few drops of cold water on it; if the water forms bubbles which dance merrily, the griddle is hot enough to bake the cakes. Grease the griddle, using an unsalted fat, unless it is a type of griddle that needs no greasing.

☼

3 Drop batter from tip of a large spoon on griddle. The spoon should hold all batter needed for one cake. Hold spoon steady and allow batter to pour in a continuous stream to make a round griddle cake. Bake a few at a time so that cakes do not touch.

☼

4 Bake on one side until cakes have puffed up and are evenly covered with bubbles. With pancake turner, turn cakes while tops are still moist and slightly set. Bake until brown on bottom. Griddle cakes should be turned only once. Serve the cakes as soon as they come from the griddle with butter and Log Cabin Syrup.

Wheat griddle cakes at their very best

ake them as they're eaten
... serve quickly
on hot, individual plates

1. A few turns of the egg beater will make batter smooth

2. When bubbles of water dance on griddle, it is ready

3. Drop batter on griddle, holding tip of spoon down

4. Turn cakes only once, browning on both sides

Here correct mixing, proper baking, and hat dependable leavener—Calumet Baking Powder—show what uality means in a griddle cake, one of the quickest of quick breads

Other Recipes Made Like Muffins

See Basic Recipe 19, Page 90

VARIATIONS OF PLAIN MUFFINS

Currant Muffins. Use recipe for Muffins (page 90), adding ½ cup currants, washed and dried, to flour mixture.

Date Muffins. Use recipe for Muffins (page 90), adding ⅔ cup dates, seeded and finely cut, to flour mixture.

Apricot Muffins. Use recipe for Muffins (page 90), adding ½ cup dried apricots, washed, dried, and cut, to flour mixture.

Nut Muffins. Use recipe for Muffins (page 90), adding ½ cup nut meats, coarsely broken, to flour mixture.

Surprise Muffins. Use recipe for Muffins (page 90). Drop a scant teaspoon of currant jelly on each muffin before baking.

✿

SPICED MUFFINS

2 cups sifted Swans Down Cake Flour   2 teaspoons Calumet Baking Powder
½ teaspoon salt   4 tablespoons sugar   ¼ teaspoon ginger
¼ teaspoon cinnamon   ¼ teaspoon cloves   ¼ teaspoon allspice
1 egg, well beaten   ¾ cup milk   4 tablespoons melted butter or other shortening

Sift flour once, measure, add baking powder, salt, sugar, and spices, and sift together three times. Combine egg, milk, and shortening. Add to flour, beating only enough to dampen all flour. Bake in greased muffin pans in hot oven (425° F.) 25 minutes, or until done. Makes 12 muffins.

✿

CORN MUFFINS

1½ cups sifted flour   2¼ teaspoons Calumet Baking Powder
2 tablespoons sugar   ¾ teaspoon salt   ¾ cup yellow corn meal
2 eggs, well beaten   1 cup milk   4 tablespoons melted butter or other shortening

Sift flour once, measure, add baking powder, sugar, and salt, and sift again. Add corn meal and mix well. Combine eggs, milk, and shortening; add to flour, stirring only enough to dampen all flour. Bake in greased muffin pans in hot oven (425° F.) 25 minutes, or until done. Makes 12 muffins. May also be baked in greased bread-stick pans.

Left-over corn muffins are delicious when split and toasted.

✿

BRAN MUFFINS

1 cup sifted flour   3½ teaspoons Calumet Baking Powder
3 tablespoons sugar   ¼ teaspoon salt   ¾ cup milk   1 cup Post's Whole Bran
1 egg, well beaten   3 tablespoons melted butter or other shortening

Sift flour once, measure, add baking powder, sugar, and salt, and sift again. Pour milk over Post's Whole Bran. Add egg and butter to bran mixture. Add flour, beating as little as possible. Bake in greased muffin pans in hot oven (425° F.) 25 minutes, or until done. Makes 8 muffins.

If desired, sour milk may be used instead of sweet, by adding ¼ teaspoon soda and using ½ teaspoon less baking powder.

SOUR MILK GRIDDLE CAKES

1 cup sifted Swans Down Cake Flour   ½ teaspoon soda   ½ teaspoon salt
1 egg, well beaten   1 cup thick sour milk or buttermilk
1 teaspoon melted butter or other shortening

Sift flour once, measure, add soda and salt, and sift again. Combine egg and milk and add to flour gradually, beating to a smooth batter. Add shortening. Bake on hot, greased griddle. Serve hot with Log Cabin Syrup, fruit jam, or maple or brown sugar. Makes 12 griddle cakes.

☼

WAFFLES

2 cups sifted Swans Down Cake Flour   2 teaspoons Calumet Baking Powder
½ teaspoon salt   3 egg yolks, well beaten
1 cup milk   4 tablespoons melted butter   3 egg whites, stiffly beaten

Sift flour once, measure, add baking powder and salt, and sift again. Combine egg yolks and milk. Add to flour, beating until smooth. Add butter. Fold in egg whites. Bake in hot waffle iron. Serve hot with Log Cabin Syrup, or creamed chicken or mushrooms. Makes four 4-section waffles. This batter may also be baked on a hot, greased griddle.

Toasted Coconut Waffles. Use recipe for Waffles (above). Sprinkle batter for each waffle with Baker's Coconut, Premium Shred, before closing iron. Serve hot with Log Cabin Syrup or butterscotch sauce.

Bacon Waffles. Use recipe for Waffles (above). Sprinkle batter for each waffle with diced uncooked bacon before closing the iron. Serve hot with scrambled eggs, or cut in strips as accompaniment for salad.

☼

CHEESE WAFFLES

2 cups sifted flour   2 teaspoons Calumet Baking Powder
½ teaspoon salt   3 egg yolks, well beaten   1¼ cups milk
5 tablespoons melted butter   1 cup grated American cheese
3 egg whites, stiffly beaten

Sift flour once, measure, add baking powder and salt, and sift again. Combine egg yolks and milk; add to flour, beating until smooth. Add butter and cheese. Fold in egg whites. Bake in hot waffle iron. Makes five 4-section waffles. This batter may also be baked on a hot, greased griddle.

☼

JELLY PANCAKES

1 cup sifted flour   1 teaspoon Calumet Baking Powder
1 teaspoon sugar   ½ teaspoon salt   1 cup milk
2 egg yolks, slightly beaten   2 tablespoons melted butter or other shortening
2 egg whites, stiffly beaten

Sift flour once, measure, add baking powder, sugar, and salt, and sift again. Combine milk and egg yolks and add to flour gradually, beating to a smooth batter. Add shortening. Fold in egg whites. Bake on hot, greased griddle. Spread with jelly and roll, or serve rolled around broiled sausages or bacon. Makes six 7-inch pancakes.

PIE CRUST

2½ cups sifted Swans Down Cake Flour
½ teaspoon salt   ⅔ cup cold shortening
⅓ cup cold water   (about)

Sift flour once, measure, add salt, and sift again.   Cut in shortening until pieces are about size of small peas. Add water
(preferably ice water), a small amount at a time, mixing
lightly with fork only enough to make flour hold together.
Continue until all flour is mixed in separate portions, neither
sticky nor crumbly. Handle as little as possible. Wrap in
waxed paper, press together, flattening slightly, and chill
thoroughly before rolling. Roll out on slightly floured board.
Bake in hot oven (450° F.) 15 minutes. Makes enough pastry
for one 9-inch two-crust pie, or fifteen 3½-inch tart shells.
Use ½ recipe for one pie shell.

Basic Recipe 21

KEY STEPS

1 How to add water to t
   flour mixture correct

2 How to roll out dough a
   keep it from stickir

3 How to line the pie pla

4 How to make attracti
   fluted rim for pie she

1 After shortening has been cut into flour, sprinkle 1 teaspoo
water over portion of mixture and toss lightly with fork—ju
enough to make it hold together, then leave it. Run fork along bo
tom of bowl with lifting motion. Add water to another portion ar
form another damp ball. Continue until mixture is formed into thes
balls. Wrap balls in waxed paper, pressing them together. Chill.

☼

2 Divide chilled dough, as necessary to roll only one crust at
time. Place dough on lightly floured board and pat out flat wit
rolling pin, pinching edge together if it cracks. Roll to ⅛-inc
thickness with light, springy touch. If pastry sticks, loosen wit
spatula and dust board lightly with flour. For a two-crust pie, ro
pastry 2 inches larger than plate; for pie shell with fluted rim, allo
another inch. Pastry cloths over pin and board facilitate rolling.

☼

3 Fit pastry loosely, yet closely, into pie plate, leaving no air bub
bles underneath. To make fluted rim, trim pastry evenly about
inch larger than pie plate. Then turn edge in and under all the wa
around and raise this double fold so that it stands up with cut-sid
against rim of plate.

☼

4 Place tip of right index finger against inner edge of fold of pas
try, then place tips of thumb and index finger of left hand o
either side and against outer edge of fold. Pinch and press dow
firmly with fingers of left hand. Continue fluting around rim.

Technic for making pastry and pie shel

*Pile a meringue lightly,
from edge in;
bake in moderate oven*

1. Add water to form dough that
is neither sticky nor dry

2. Roll chilled pastry, pinching
edge together if it cracks

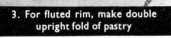

3. For fluted rim, make double
upright fold of pastry

4. Your fingers can make a pretty
fluted rim in no time

Use cold ingredients and handle as little as
possible—these are two rules of pastry making. Above see just how
to follow these rules, and how to add an expert's touch to your pies

CHERRY PIE

2½ tablespoons Minute Tapioca   1 cup sugar
3½ cups red cherries and juice   1 tablespoon melted butter
¼ teaspoon salt   1 recipe Calumet Pie Crust (page 101)

Combine Minute Tapioca, sugar, cherries, butter, and salt and let stand 15 minutes, or while pastry is being made. Line a 9-inch pie plate with ½ of pastry rolled ⅛ inch thick, allowing pastry to extend ½ inch beyond edge of plate. Moisten edge and fold inward, even with rim of plate. Moisten edge again. Fill with cherry mixture. Roll other half of pastry to ⅛-inch thickness. Fold and cut slits to permit escape of steam. Place upper crust on filled lower one, opening out folded half and drawing snugly across top. Press edges together. Trim off surplus pastry. Bake in hot oven (450° F.) 15 minutes; decrease to 350° F.; bake 30 minutes. *Basic Recipe 22*

KEY STEPS

1 How to line pie plate and trim the lower crust

2 How to make rim-pocket

3 How to fit upper crust and seal filling in pie

4 When and how to trim upper crust of filled pie

1 Roll chilled pastry a generous 2 inches larger than pie plate to allow for sinking down into plate and for making a double fold at edge. Fold in half, lift carefully, and place across ungreased pie plate with fold in center. Allow pastry to sink down into plate, then unfold and fit into place without stretching pastry. Trim pastry allowing it to hang over sides of pie plate about ½ inch.

☼

2 Moisten edge of pastry, brushing lightly around the rim with cold water. Then fold the little curtain of dough up and over so that cut edge is on top and rolled edge is just inside outer rim of pie plate. Do not press it down, just fold it over to form a little ½-inch pocket on rim of plate, open toward the center. This little pocket helps to keep the juice from boiling out of the edges of the pie. Place the cherry mixture in the pie. No soaked undercrust this time! Minute Tapioca absorbs a large part of the juice and keeps it in the pie.

☼

3 Moisten outer edge of lower crust with cold water just before fitting top crust. If the top crust is folded as shown, there is little danger of its breaking when it is placed upon filled pie. Slits are cut in upper crust to allow the steam to escape.

☼

4 Fit two crusts together, pressing lightly so as not to tear pastry. Trim off top crust, being careful not to cut open the little rim-pocket of under crust. Hold knife as shown. Last of all, with fingers or with tines of a fork dipped in flour, press edges of two crusts together to make a tight seal all around the pie.

The proper way with two-crust fruit pie

*Crust tender and flaky
. . . golden brown
and all juice in the pie*

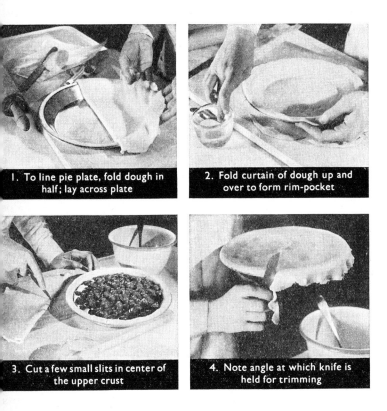

1. To line pie plate, fold dough in half; lay across plate

2. Fold curtain of dough up and over to form rim-pocket

3. Cut a few small slits in center of the upper crust

4. Note angle at which knife is held for trimming

In which some tricks are shown for keeping fruit juices in the pie and out of the oven during baking. The art of fitting and trimming both upper and lower crusts is pictured also

PASTRY SHELLS

Pie Shell. Use ½ recipe Pie Crust, lining 9-inch pie plate with pastry, according to directions on page 96. To bake, prick pastry with fork, or line with waxed paper and fill with beans or rice during first few minutes of baking to hold shape. Bake in hot oven (450° F.) 15 minutes.

Tart Shells. Roll pastry to ⅛-inch thickness. Cut with 5-inch floured cooky cutter; fit carefully on outside of upturned tart or muffin pans. Trim edges. Prick with fork. Bake in hot oven (450° F.) 10 to 15 minutes.

✿

LEMON MERINGUE PIE

½ cup Swans Down Cake Flour   1¼ cups sugar   Dash of salt
1½ cups water   3 egg yolks, slightly beaten   ½ cup lemon juice
1 tablespoon grated lemon rind   1 baked 9-inch pie shell

3 egg whites   6 tablespoons sugar

Combine flour, sugar, and salt in top of double boiler. Add water and egg yolks, mixing thoroughly. Place over hot water and cook 10 minutes, stirring constantly. Remove from fire; add lemon juice and rind. Cool. Pour into pie shell. Beat egg whites until foamy throughout. Add sugar, 2 tablespoons at a time, beating after each addition until sugar is blended. When all sugar is added, continue beating until mixture stands in peaks. Pile lightly on filling. Bake in moderate oven (350° F.) 15 minutes.

✿

VANITY FAIR COCONUT CUSTARD PIE

½ recipe Pie Crust (page 96)   3 eggs, slightly beaten
⅛ teaspoon salt   ½ cup sugar   3 cups milk, scalded
1 cup Baker's Coconut, Premium Shred

Line pie plate with pastry, rolled to ⅛-inch thickness, allowing pastry to extend 1 inch beyond edge. Fit loosely on plate. Fold edge back to form standing rim and flute with fingers. Combine eggs, salt, and sugar; add milk gradually, then add coconut, and mix thoroughly. Pour into pie shell. Bake in hot oven (450° F.) 20 minutes, then decrease heat to moderate (350° F.) and bake 15 minutes longer. Cool.

✿

BANANA PIE SUPRÊME

6 tablespoons Swans Down Cake Flour   ⅔ cup sugar   ¼ teaspoon salt
1¾ cups milk   2 egg yolks, slightly beaten   1¼ teaspoons vanilla
½ cup cream, whipped   3 bananas   1 baked 9-inch pie shell

Mix together flour, sugar, and salt in top of double boiler. Add milk and cook over hot water, stirring constantly, until mixture thickens. Then cook 15 minutes longer, stirring occasionally. Pour a small amount of mixture over egg yolks, beating vigorously; return to double boiler, and cook 2 minutes longer, stirring constantly. Remove from fire. Cool. Add vanilla. Chill. Fold in whipped cream. Arrange cream filling and sliced bananas in layers in pie shell. Garnish with whipped cream and banana slices.

CALUMET PIE CRUST

2½ cups sifted flour   ¼ teaspoon **Calumet Baking Powder**   ½ teaspoon salt
⅔ cup cold shortening   ⅓ cup cold water (about)

Sift flour once, measure, add baking powder, and salt, and sift again. Cut in shortening until pieces are about size of small peas. Add water (preferably ice water), a small amount at a time, mixing lightly with fork. Handle as little as possible. Wrap in waxed paper and chill thoroughly before rolling. Roll out on slightly floured board. Bake in hot oven (450° F.) 15 minutes. Makes enough pastry for one 9-inch two-crust pie, or fifteen 3½-inch tart shells. Use ½ recipe for one pie shell only.

Two-crust Pie. Line 9-inch pie plate with ½ recipe Calumet Pie Crust (above), rolled to ⅛-inch thickness. Moisten edges of the pastry with cold water. Fill pie shell. Roll other half of pastry to ⅛-inch thickness. Fold half the pastry back on other half. With sharp knife make several slits to permit escape of steam. Place upper crust on filled lower one, opening out folded half after it is placed on pie. Press edges together with fork dipped in flour, then with sharp knife trim off surplus pastry. Brush with milk or beaten egg white, if a slight glaze is desired. Bake in hot oven (425° F. to 450° F.) 10 to 15 minutes; then decrease heat to moderate (350° F.) and bake until pastry is browned, and filling is done.

☼

FRUIT PIES

Fresh rhubarb, peach, grape, or berry pie. Combine 3½ cups prepared fruit, 1½ to 2 tablespoons Minute Tapioca, 1 to 1¼ cups sugar, ¼ teaspoon salt, and 1 tablespoon melted butter. Let stand 15 minutes, or while pastry is being made. Use as filling for 9-inch two-crust pie.

Canned peach, plum, pineapple, cherry, or berry pie. Combine 2½ cups canned fruit (drained), 1 cup fruit juice, 2½ tablespoons Minute Tapioca, sugar to sweeten, ⅛ teaspoon salt, and 1 tablespoon melted butter. Let stand 15 minutes, or while pastry is being made. Use as filling for 9-inch two-crust or crisscross pie. Minute Tapioca in fruit pies keeps the juice in the pie and prevents it from running out into the oven.

☼

CRISSCROSS APRICOT PIE

1½ tablespoons Minute Tapioca   ⅓ cup sugar   ¼ teaspoon salt
1 tablespoon melted butter   2 cups cooked dried apricots, drained
½ cup canned crushed pineapple, drained   1 cup apricot juice
½ cup pineapple juice   1 recipe Pie Crust (page 96)

Combine Minute Tapioca, sugar, salt, butter, fruit, and fruit juices and let stand 15 minutes, or while pastry is being made. Line a 9-inch pie plate with about ½ of pastry, rolled to ⅛-inch thickness, allowing pastry to extend 1 inch beyond edge. Fold edge back to form standing rim. Fill with apricot mixture. Moisten edge of pie with cold water and arrange lattice of pastry strips across top. Flute rim with fingers. Bake in hot oven (425° F.) 10 minutes; then decrease heat to moderate (350° F.) and bake 30 minutes longer. Cool. Serve with or without whipped cream.

Frosting—
The Festive Finish for Cake

※

FROSTING is the crowning touch to cakes of beauty and distinction, the last act in that interesting performance of making a cake that is a joy both to behold and to eat.

Since a cooked frosting is the most versatile and popular of all frostings, yet one which often presents difficulties, the frostings in this book are organized around a Basic Recipe for Seven Minute Frosting (page 104). This lovely frosting is very easy to work with —it stays soft, and molds and swirls beautifully. When you have mastered it you are ready to give any cake a beautiful finish.

Seven Minute Frosting lends itself to many variations, several of which are represented in the supplementary recipes which accompany it (page 106). Still more may be had by adding a bit of grated lemon or orange rind, sprinkling with coconut, or chopped nuts, spreading with a film of melted, unsweetened chocolate.

On pages 107, 108, and 109 are grouped other types of frostings— butter frostings, cooked fondant frostings, special chocolate frostings, and some novelty frostings—an assortment which makes an infinite variety of fine cake combinations possible.

Cake Decorating for Special Occasions

On certain occasions you may want to decorate your cakes, may want to give them an ultra-festive air, or a little special formality.

Simplicity should be the keynote of such decorations. A second principle is that cake decorations should be edible and appropriate. Suitable materials to use are white coconut or tinted coconut, pistachios, walnuts, pecans, almonds, raisins, currants, strips of angelica, bits of candied fruit, preserved ginger, dots of bright jelly, tiny colored or silver candies, and tiny chocolate candies.

Cakes to be decorated should be frosted in the usual way. Then, with the design well in mind, let the borders of the decoration follow the shape of the cake. Arrange any flower or special motifs at intervals of thirds, fifths, or sevenths, around the cake, provided the cake is circular—or in the corners, if it is square.

Butter frostings are often used in a pastry bag, as they hold their shape. The tube is much more efficient if only half filled.

Delicately tinted frostings are a dainty variation, and fit nicely into menus of definite color schemes. They may be made by adding a small amount of coloring to any white frosting, and blending it evenly before spreading. Be careful not to use too much coloring for highly colored frostings do not look well and are unappetizing.

Of such cake do cooks dream.
High and light and airy cake, with a velvety crumb
and an expert touch in the frosting and decorating

For your parties—silhouette cake

SEVEN MINUTE FROSTING

2 egg whites, unbeaten   1½ cups sugar
5 tablespoons water
1½ teaspoons light corn syrup   1 teaspoon vanilla

Combine egg whites, sugar, water, and corn syrup in top of
double boiler, beating with rotary egg beater until thoroughly
mixed. Place over rapidly boiling water, beat constantly with
rotary egg beater and cook 7 minutes, or until frosting will
stand in peaks. Remove from boiling water; add vanilla and
beat until thick enough to spread. Makes enough frosting to
cover tops and sides of two 9-inch layers, or top and sides of
8x8x2-inch cake (generously), or about 2 dozen cup cakes.
This frosting may be varied by folding in chopped nut meats,
Baker's Coconut, or pieces of dried or candied fruit, or by
tinting delicately with colorings. *Basic Recipe 23*

KEY STEPS

1 How to beat over boil
ing water—when to sto

2 How to beat while cool
ing—and when to sto

3 How to spread frostin
between the cake layer

4 How to frost the outsid

1 You need a deep double boiler and a sturdy rotary egg beate
for making this frosting. Keep water in lower part boiling rap
idly, and beat frosting constantly. It thickens as it cooks. In abou
7 minutes (if you have a strong beater) the frosting will stand up i
soft, snowy peaks when you lift the beater.

☼

2 As soon as the frosting stands in peaks, remove top of doubl
boiler from over hot water. Add flavoring and continue beating
With each whirl of the beater the mixture becomes thicker and
fluffier. Stop beating when the frosting will hold firm little swirls o
ridges as it falls back from the beater. At this stage it is cool and
thick enough to spread.

☼

3 Have the cake cold and free from loose crumbs before attempt
ing to frost it. The frosting should be cool so that it does not ru
or soak into the cake. Put frosting on bottom layer, spreading i
smoothly with a spatula or knife. Keep the edges of the cake even
Arrange layers so that cake, when frosted, is uniform in height.

☼

4 Frost sides of cake first, starting over edge at top and spreading
the soft frosting lightly over the edge and around the sides o
cake with sweeping strokes of the spatula. Then pile more ribbonlike folds in center top, and work the frosting out lightly to edges
Swirl frosting into snowy ridges with back of silver spoon.

An easy, sure method for cooked frosting

*Last but not the least
the frosting—
crowning glory of all*

1. Beat over boiling water until peaks hold from beater

2. Add flavoring and beat until thick enough to spread

3. Spread frosting carefully on lower layer; fit top

4. Frost cake quickly, using light, but deft strokes

In which there are shown, step by step, the ost important points about making a soft cooked frosting. Some nts on how to frost a cake artfully and easily are given here also

CHOCOLATE SEVEN MINUTE FROSTING

Use recipe for Seven Minute Frosting (page 104). Fold in 3 squares Baker's Unsweetened Chocolate, melted and cooled, with vanilla. Do not beat.

☼

BURNT SUGAR FROSTING

Use recipe for Seven Minute Frosting (page 104), substituting 2 tablespoons caramelized sugar syrup (page 42) for vanilla in recipe.

☼

HARVEST MOON FROSTING

2 egg whites, unbeaten   1 cup brown sugar, firmly packed   Dash of salt
¼ cup water   1 teaspoon vanilla
¾ cup almonds, blanched, chopped, and toasted

Combine egg whites, sugar, salt, and water in top of double boiler, beating with rotary egg beater until thoroughly mixed. Place over rapidly boiling water, beat constantly with rotary egg beater, and cook 7 minutes, or until frosting will stand in peaks. Remove from boiling water; add vanilla and beat until thick enough to spread. Add nuts. Makes enough frosting to cover tops and sides of two 9-inch layers, or one 8x8x2-inch cake.

☼

LEMON SEVEN MINUTE FROSTING

3 egg whites, unbeaten   2¼ cups sugar   6 tablespoons water
1 tablespoon light corn syrup   2 teaspoons lemon juice

Combine egg whites, sugar, water, and corn syrup in top of double boiler, beating with rotary egg beater until thoroughly mixed. Place over rapidly boiling water, beat constantly with rotary egg beater, and cook 7 minutes, or until frosting will stand in peaks. Remove from boiling water. Beat until slightly thickened and add lemon juice. Continue beating until thick enough to spread. Makes enough frosting to cover tops and sides of four 9-inch layers, or tops and sides of two 8x8x2-inch cakes.

☼

MACAROON FROSTING AND FILLING

2 egg whites, unbeaten   1½ cups sugar   2 teaspoons light corn syrup
4½ tablespoons water   ¼ teaspoon almond extract
Rose coloring   6 macaroons, dried, rolled, and sifted

Combine egg whites, sugar, corn syrup, and water in top of double boiler, beating with rotary egg beater until thoroughly mixed. Place over rapidly boiling water, beat constantly with rotary egg beater, and cook 7 minutes, or until frosting will stand in peaks. Remove from boiling water; add almond extract and rose coloring to make a delicate tint. Beat until nearly thick enough to spread. For filling, add enough frosting to macaroon crumbs to make a filling that will spread easily. Spread between layers. Spread remaining frosting on top and sides of cake. Makes enough to cover tops and sides of two 9-inch layers, or 15 Little Baltimore Cakes (page 43).

BUTTER FROSTING

4 tablespoons butter	2 cups sifted confectioners' sugar
3 tablespoons milk (about)	1 teaspoon vanilla Dash of salt

Cream butter; add part of sugar gradually, blending after each addition. Add remaining sugar, alternately with milk, until of right consistency to spread. Beat after each addition until smooth. Add vanilla and salt. Makes enough frosting to cover tops of two 9-inch layers, or top and sides of 8x8x2-inch cake, or about 2 dozen cup cakes.

✿

ORANGE BUTTER FROSTING

1 tablespoon grated orange rind	½ teaspoon grated lemon rind
4 tablespoons orange juice	2 teaspoons lemon juice
3 tablespoons butter 1 egg yolk, unbeaten	⅛ teaspoon salt
3 cups sifted confectioners' sugar	

Add orange and lemon rind to fruit juice and let stand 10 minutes; strain if desired. Cream butter; add egg yolk and salt and mix well. Add part of sugar gradually, blending after each addition. Add remaining sugar, alternately with fruit juice, until of right consistency to spread. Beat after each addition until smooth. Makes enough frosting to cover tops and sides of two 9-inch layers, or top and sides of 8x8x2-inch cake (generously).

✿

LUSCIOUS LEMON FROSTING

1 tablespoon grated orange rind	3 tablespoons butter
3 cups sifted confectioners' sugar 2 tablespoons lemon juice	1 tablespoon water
Dash of salt	

Add orange rind to butter; cream well. Add part of sugar gradually, blending after each addition. Combine lemon juice and water; add to creamed mixture, alternately with remaining sugar, until of right consistency to spread. Beat after each addition until smooth. Add salt. Makes enough frosting to cover tops and sides of two 9-inch layers, or top and sides of 8x8x2-inch cake (generously), or about 3 dozen cup cakes.

✿

BOILED FROSTING

1½ cups sugar	½ teaspoon light corn syrup
⅔ cup boiling water 2 egg whites, stiffly beaten	1 teaspoon vanilla

Combine sugar, corn syrup, and water. Bring quickly to a boil, stirring only until sugar is dissolved. Boil rapidly, without stirring, until small amount of syrup forms a soft ball in cold water, or spins a long thread when dropped from tip of spoon (240° F.). Pour syrup in fine stream over egg whites, beating constantly. Add vanilla. Continue beating with rotary egg beater 10 to 15 minutes, or until frosting is cool and of right consistency to spread. Use wooden spoon when too stiff for beater. Makes enough frosting to cover tops and sides of two 9-inch layers, or top and sides of 8x8x2-inch cake (generously), or about 2 dozen cup cakes.

CLEVER JUDY FROSTING

1 cup sifted confectioners' sugar   1 egg or 2 egg yolks   ¼ cup milk
½ teaspoon vanilla   2 to 4 squares Baker's Unsweetened Chocolate, melted
1 tablespoon softened butter

Combine ingredients in order given, beating with rotary egg beater unti
blended. Place bowl in pan of cracked ice or ice water and continue beat
ing until of right consistency to spread (about 3 minutes). Makes enoug
frosting to cover tops of two 9-inch layers, or top and sides of 8x8x2
inch cake, or about 2 dozen cup cakes.

✿

HUNGARIAN CHOCOLATE FROSTING AND FILLING

4 squares Baker's Unsweetened Chocolate
1 cup confectioners' sugar   2 tablespoons hot water
2 eggs   6 tablespoons butter

Melt chocolate in double boiler. Remove from boiling water, add suga
and water, and blend. Add eggs, one at a time, beating well after eac
addition. Add butter, one-third at a time, beating thoroughly after eac
amount. Makes enough frosting and filling to cover tops of two 9-inc
layers, or top and sides of 8x8x2-inch cake, or about 2 dozen cup cake

✿

CHOCOLATE BUTTER FROSTING

4 tablespoons butter   2 cups sifted confectioners' sugar
½ teaspoon vanilla   Dash of salt
1½ squares Baker's Unsweetened Chocolate, melted   3 tablespoons milk (about)

Cream butter; add part of sugar gradually, blending after each additior
Add vanilla, salt, and chocolate and mix well. Add remaining sugar, alter
nately with milk, until of right consistency to spread. Beat after eac
addition until smooth. Makes enough frosting to cover tops of two 9-inc
layers, or top and sides of 8x8x2-inch cake, or about 2 dozen cup cake
This frosting may be flavored with grated orange rind, if desired.

✿

FUDGE FROSTING

3 squares Baker's Unsweetened Chocolate, cut in pieces
1½ cups milk   3 cups sugar   Dash of salt
3 tablespoons light corn syrup   3 tablespoons butter   1½ teaspoons vanilla

Add chocolate to milk and place over low flame. Cook until mixture i
smooth and blended, stirring constantly. Add sugar, salt, and corn syrup
stir until sugar is dissolved and mixture boils. Continue cooking, withou
stirring, until a small amount of mixture forms a very soft ball in col
water (232° F.). Remove from fire. Add butter and vanilla. Cool to luke
warm (110° F.). Beat until of right consistency to spread. If desired, plac
over hot water to keep soft while spreading. Makes enough frosting t
cover tops and sides of two 9-inch layers, or top and sides of 8x8x2-incl
cake, or about 2 dozen cup cakes.

COFFEE FROSTING

3 tablespoons butter   2 cups sifted confectioners' sugar
2 tablespoons strong coffee (about)   Dash of salt

Cream butter; add part of sugar gradually, blending after each addition. Add remaining sugar, alternately with coffee, until of right consistency to spread. Beat after each addition until smooth. Add salt. Makes enough frosting to cover 8x8x2-inch cake, or tops of two 9-inch layers.

☼

CREOLE BUTTER FROSTING

1½ tablespoons butter   2 cups sifted confectioners' sugar
1 tablespoon Baker's Breakfast Cocoa   ⅛ teaspoon salt
3½ tablespoons strong coffee (about)   1 teaspoon vanilla

Cream butter. Sift sugar, cocoa, and salt together. Add part of sugar mixture gradually to butter, blending after each addition. Add remaining sugar mixture, alternately with coffee, until of right consistency to spread. Beat after each addition until smooth. Add vanilla. Makes enough frosting to cover tops of two 9-inch layers, or top and sides of 8x8x2-inch cake.

☼

CARAMEL FROSTING

1½ cups brown sugar, firmly packed   1½ cups granulated sugar
1½ cups milk   2 tablespoons butter

Combine sugars and milk and bring to a boil, stirring constantly. Then cook, without stirring, until a small amount of syrup forms a very soft ball in cold water (232° F.). Add butter and remove from fire. Cool to lukewarm (110° F.); beat until thick and creamy and of right consistency to spread. If desired, place over hot water to keep soft while spreading. Makes enough frosting to cover tops and sides of two 9-inch layers, or top and sides of 8x8x2-inch cake, or about 2 dozen cup cakes.

☼

LADY BALTIMORE FROSTING AND FILLING

1½ cups sugar   ½ teaspoon light corn syrup   ⅔ cup boiling water
2 egg whites, stiffly beaten   1 teaspoon vanilla   6 figs, chopped
½ cup raisins, chopped   ½ cup pecan or walnut meats, chopped

Combine sugar, corn syrup, and water. Bring quickly to a boil, stirring only until sugar is dissolved. Boil rapidly, without stirring, until a small amount of syrup forms a soft ball in cold water, or spins a long thread when dropped from tip of spoon (240° F.). Pour syrup in fine stream over egg whites, beating constantly. Add vanilla. Continue beating with a rotary egg beater 10 to 15 minutes, or until frosting is cool and of right consistency to spread. Use wooden spoon when too stiff for beater. For filling, add enough frosting to fruit and nuts to make a filling that will spread easily. Spread between layers. Spread remaining frosting on top and sides of cake. Makes enough filling and frosting to spread between layers and on top and sides of Lady Baltimore Cake (page 44).

Some Bright New Menu Ideas
For the Hostess

✿

THESE fine, light cakes, these proud biscuits, and melt-in-your-mouth pies you've been learning to make deserve attractive settings. Proper, pleasing table service is the last but not the least chapter in the art of home baking.

So this little book comes to an end with some suggestions to the hostess, ranging from a hint or two on the arrangement of the table for a formal luncheon to the packing of a picnic basket. The everyday needs have been remembered, too. Many an idea is offered to the homemaker wise enough to be a real hostess to her family.

The hostess suggestions in the following pages consist of carefully planned menus for certain occasions, with illustrations of some feature of table service. The first, Menu Suggestion 1 (page 112), has to do with an impromptu guest luncheon, for example—a simple meal, yet smartly served. On the opposite page (page 113) is the more elaborate springtime luncheon, Menu Suggestion 2, showing its attractive dessert service. Following are two pages of recipes (pages 114 and 115), one for each menu suggestion. In this way the section continues.

Recipes for many of the dishes featured in these menus are found on the pages which directly follow the menu suggestions or are taken from the basic recipe section of the book. A footnote on each menu refers you to the correct recipe pages.

Each hostess suggestion is built around an occasion. Much of the story, in every case, is told in the illustration. The picture method has been used here, as in the rest of the book, as far as possible.

Some Well-planned Menus

To serve meals which delight as well as satisfy is a challenge to the most competent of hostesses. It demands skill in the preparation of food, wisdom in its selection, imagination about its service, and real executive ability.

Good meals should appeal to the eye almost as much as to the taste. They should present interesting contrasts of flavor, texture, color, and shape, a nice balance between substantial and light foods, and should be so planned that they can be served without fuss or flurry. Many are the considerations which go into the planning of an adequate, suitable, enjoyable menu: the cost, the needs of the particular situation, the help you will have in serving it, the cooking processes you wish to use. The hostess suggestions offered here furnish many an answer to your daily meal-planning problems

A simple dessert, yet fit for royalty.
This rich, fragrant gingerbread, fresh from the oven,
served with tart, baked apples and cold sweet milk

Gingerbread—an all-time favorite

An informal luncheon may be as attractive as formal affair if the sam regard is shown for it appearance and prepara tion. This table is set wit inexpensive but smar glass and china. Eac place is carefully ar ranged, for looks an comfort. The salad is con veniently placed at th right, since no beverag is served with this cours

MENU SUGGESTION 1

SCALLOPED SALMON
SLICED CUCUMBERS AND WATER CRESS WITH FRENCH DRESSING
*GRAHAM NUT MUFFINS
*GINGERBREAD UPSIDE DOWN CAKE
TEA OR COFFEE

✿

CLEAR TOMATO SOUP
*CHEESE DROP BISCUITS   FRUIT SALAD
*SPICE SQUARES WITH MOLASSES WHIPPED CREAM   TEA

Graham Nut Muffins and Gingerbread Upside Down Cake round out and give character to an otherwise very light, economical meal. To another menu Cheese Biscuits and Spice Squares give similar aid.

Recipes for dishes marked [*] are on pages 82 and 114.

Two impromptu guest luncheons

*A more formal luncheon
ending proudly with
tarts and coffee*

Apple blossoms for a centerpiece furnish the lovely decoration for this springtime luncheon. It's a party occasion, ending with dessert formally served on the very best plates, and coffee poured at the table. The dainty luncheon cloth with the gleaming silver, the candies, to be passed at the end of the meal, all add to the glamorous picture.

MENU SUGGESTION 2

CONSOMMÉ

PAPRIKA CRACKERS   GREEN OLIVES

GRILLED SWEETBREADS ON TOAST POINTS

NEW ASPARAGUS WITH HOLLANDAISE SAUCE

*NOVELTY ROLLS OR *LEMON BISCUITS

WATERMELON CIRCLES

*FRESH STRAWBERRY TARTS OR *RIBBON CAKE

PASTEL CANDIES

COFFEE

What could be more appropriate or more festive for dessert than these Fresh Strawberry Tarts? They sustain the guests' interest even after such very tempting fare as sweetbreads and asparagus.

Recipes for dishes marked [*] are on pages 42 and 115.

A delicious springtime luncheon

GRAHAM NUT MUFFINS

1 cup sifted flour   1 cup Graham flour   3 teaspoons Calumet Baking Powder
½ cup sugar   1 teaspoon salt   ½ cup walnut meats, coarsely broken
1 egg, well beaten   1 cup milk
4 tablespoons melted butter or other shortening

Sift flour once, measure, add Graham flour, baking powder, sugar, and salt, and sift again. Add walnuts and mix. Combine egg, milk, and shortening. Add to flour, beating only enough to dampen all flour. Bake in greased muffin pans in hot oven (425° F.) 25 minutes. Makes 18.

✿

GINGERBREAD
(1 egg)

2 cups sifted Swans Down Cake Flour   2 teaspoons Calumet Baking Powder
¼ teaspoon soda   2 teaspoons ginger   1 teaspoon cinnamon
½ teaspoon salt   ⅓ cup butter or other shortening   ½ cup sugar
1 egg, well beaten   ⅔ cup molasses
¾ cup sour milk or buttermilk

Sift flour once, measure, add baking powder, soda, spices, and salt, and sift together three times. Cream butter thoroughly, add sugar gradually, and cream together until light and fluffy. Add egg and molasses; then flour, alternately with milk, a small amount at a time. Beat after each addition until smooth. Bake in greased pan, 8x8x2 inches, in moderate oven (350° F.) 50 minutes, or until done.

✿

GINGERBREAD UPSIDE DOWN CAKE

Prepare batter for Gingerbread (above). Melt 2 tablespoons butter in an 8x8x2-inch pan. Add ½ cup molasses and ¼ cup raisins. Heat over low flame. Blend and arrange 2 apples, pared, cored, and thinly sliced, to cover surface of molasses mixture. Pour batter over contents of pan. Bake in moderate oven (350° F.) 50 minutes, or until done. Serve upside down.

✿

SPICE SQUARES WITH MOLASSES WHIPPED CREAM
(2 eggs)

2½ cups sifted Swans Down Cake Flour   ½ teaspoon soda
2 teaspoons Calumet Baking Powder   ¼ teaspoon allspice   ¼ teaspoon mace
¼ teaspoon nutmeg   ½ teaspoon cloves   2 teaspoons cinnamon
½ cup butter or other shortening   1 cup brown sugar, firmly packed
2 eggs, well beaten   1 cup sour milk or buttermilk

Sift flour once, measure, add soda, baking powder, and spices, and sift together three times. Cream butter thoroughly, add sugar gradually, and cream together until light and fluffy. Add eggs, mixing well; then flour mixture, alternately with milk, a small amount at a time. Beat after each addition until smooth. Bake in a greased pan, 8x8x2 inches, in moderate oven (350° F.) for 50 minutes. Serve in squares with Molasses Whipped Cream made by folding 2 tablespoons molasses into ½ cup cream, whipped.

NOVELTY ROLLS

2 cups sifted Swans Down Cake Flour   2 teaspoons Calumet Baking Powder
½ teaspoon salt   1 tablespoon butter or other shortening   ⅔ cup milk

Melted butter   Caraway or poppy seeds

Sift flour once, measure, add baking powder and salt, and sift again. Cut in shortening; add milk all at once and stir carefully until all flour is dampened. Then stir vigorously until mixture forms a soft dough and follows spoon around bowl. Turn out immediately on slightly floured board and knead lightly 2 to 3 minutes. Roll ¼ inch thick. Cut in crescents with 2-inch floured biscuit cutter, or roll into strips, 6x½ inches, and tie in knot. Brush tops with melted butter and sprinkle with caraway or poppy seeds. (Mixture of 1 tablespoon sugar and ⅛ teaspoon cinnamon may be used in place of seeds.) Place in greased pan; cover and let rise in warm place 20 minutes. Bake in hot oven (425° F.) 10 minutes. Again butter tops, dropping melted butter from teaspoon, and continue baking 5 to 10 minutes. Remove from oven and butter tops as before. Makes 16.

✿

LEMON BISCUITS

2 cups sifted Swans Down Cake Flour   2 teaspoons Calumet Baking Powder
½ teaspoon salt   4 tablespoons butter or other shortening
1½ teaspoons grated lemon rind   ⅔ cup milk

4 tablespoons sugar   1½ teaspoons grated lemon rind
¼ teaspoon lemon juice (about)

Sift flour once, measure, add baking powder and salt, and sift again. Cut in shortening; add lemon rind and blend. Add milk all at once and stir carefully until all flour is dampened. Then stir vigorously until mixture forms a soft dough and follows spoon around bowl. Turn out immediately on slightly floured board and knead 30 seconds. Roll ¼ inch thick and cut with 1½-inch floured biscuit cutter. Combine sugar, lemon rind, and enough lemon juice to make a crumbly mixture. Place half of biscuits in greased muffin pans, spread with melted butter and with sugar mixture, and top with remaining biscuits, pressing lightly together. Bake in hot oven (450° F.) 8 to 10 minutes, or until done. Makes 2½ dozen biscuits.

✿

FRESH STRAWBERRY TARTS

1 quart strawberries, washed and hulled   1 cup sugar
1 package Strawberry Jell-O   1 cup warm water   1 cup cream, whipped
9 baked 3½-inch tart shells

Combine strawberries and sugar and let stand 10 minutes. Dissolve Jell-O in warm water. Pour over strawberries. Chill until Jell-O begins to thicken. Fold 4 tablespoons thickened Jell-O into whipped cream. Chill. Place layer of whipped cream in bottom of each tart shell. Chill about 10 minutes. Cover with layer of jellied strawberries, pressing hull-end of each strawberry lightly into cream. Add thickened Jell-O to fill tart. Chill a few minutes longer and serve.

*A smart bridge luncheon
may be served easily
on small tables*

Even the small hous
is able to accommodate
number of luncheo
guests if the menu
planned so that it may b
served on the card table.
And very smart it is t
give a bridge luncheo
this way. To simplify th
service, the rolls may b
buttered and served wit
the salad, coffee passe
in the cups, and the des
sert placed on the tabl

MENU SUGGESTION 3

CREAM OF MUSHROOM SOUP

FROZEN CHEESE SALAD

FRUIT MAYONNAISE

*CALUMET POCKETBOOK ROLLS OR *APRICOT MUFFINS

*COCONUT ORANGE ROLL OR *SPICE DROPS

COFFEE OR FRUIT PUNCH

PEPPERMINTS

Calumet Pocketbook Rolls, served piping hot, are just the right
contrast and supplement to a Frozen Cheese Salad. With the dessert of Coconut Orange Roll offer a second cup of coffee.

Recipes for dishes marked [*] are on pages 94 and 118.

For the luncheon with bridge

Let waffles, baked at the table, be the feature of a supper or luncheon for your friends. There is a fascination about watching the creamy waffle batter poured into the waffle iron, about waiting until—presto! out comes the waffle, crisp, brown, fragrant. The supper or luncheon may be built around a main dish waffle or around a dessert waffle.

MENU SUGGESTION 4

*CHEESE WAFFLES WITH BACON	WALDORF SALAD
GRILLED TOMATOES	CHEESE DREAMS OLIVES
*DATE STICKS	*SUMMER DESSERT WAFFLES
FRUIT COFFEE	COFFEE

☼

*WAFFLES WITH CREAMED MUSHROOMS
CRANBERRY JELLY   CELERY CURLS
*OLD-FASHIONED NUT LOAF OR *BROWNIES
JELLIED GRAPEFRUIT   COFFEE

Waffles with mushrooms or Cheese Waffles are popular for the main course; Summer Dessert Waffles, a suggestion for the end of the meal. One or two light dishes, and a beverage, complete these menus.

Recipes for dishes marked [*] are on pages 95 and 119.

The waffle supper or luncheon

CALUMET POCKETBOOK ROLLS

2 cups sifted Swans Down Cake Flour
2 teaspoons Calumet Baking Powder ½ teaspoon salt
1 tablespoon butter or other shortening ⅔ cup milk

Sift flour once, measure, add baking powder and salt, and sift again. Cut
in shortening; add milk all at once and stir carefully until all flour is
dampened. Then stir vigorously until mixture forms a soft dough and follows spoon around bowl. Turn out immediately on well floured board and
knead lightly 2 to 3 minutes. Roll ¼ inch thick. Cut with 2-inch floured
biscuit cutter. Fold double and press edges together lightly. Place in
greased pan; brush tops with melted butter. Cover and let rise in warm
place 20 minutes. Bake in hot oven (425° F.) 10 minutes. Again brush tops
with melted butter and continue baking 5 to 10 minutes longer. Remove
from oven and brush tops with melted butter. Makes 18 rolls.

Knots. Use recipe for Calumet Pocketbook Rolls (above). Roll dough ¼
inch thick on slightly floured board and cut in strips, 6x½ inches. Tie
each in loose knot. Place in greased pan; brush tops with melted butter.
Cover, let rise in warm place 20 minutes, and bake as directed.

✿

SPICE DROPS

2¼ cups sifted Swans Down Cake Flour 1½ teaspoons Calumet Baking Powder
½ teaspoon soda ¼ teaspoon salt ¼ teaspoon nutmeg
¼ teaspoon allspice ½ cup butter or other shortening
⅔ cup brown sugar, firmly packed 1 egg, unbeaten
½ cup walnut meats, broken ½ cup raisins ½ cup heavy sour cream

Sift flour once, measure, add baking powder, soda, salt, and spices, and sift
together three times. Cream butter thoroughly, add sugar gradually, and
cream together until light and fluffy. Add egg and beat well; then add nuts
and raisins and mix well. Add flour, alternately with sour cream, beating
after each addition until smooth. Drop from teaspoon on ungreased baking
sheet and bake in hot oven (425° F.) 8 to 10 minutes, or until delicately
browned. Makes 3½ dozen cookies. Broken pecan meats may be substituted
for walnuts in this recipe, if desired.

✿

COCONUT ORANGE ROLL

Use recipe for Old-fashioned Jelly Roll (page 72), spreading cake with
Coconut Orange Filling instead of jelly.

Coconut Orange Filling

4 tablespoons Swans Down Cake Flour ½ cup sugar Dash of salt
⅓ cup orange juice 3 tablespoons lemon juice 2 tablespoons water
1 egg, well beaten 2 tablespoons butter 1½ teaspoons grated orange rind
¼ cup Baker's Coconut, Premium Shred, finely cut

Combine flour, sugar, and salt in top of double boiler; add fruit juice,
water, and egg. Place over rapidly boiling water and cook 10 minutes, or
until thickened, stirring constantly. Remove from boiling water; add butter, orange rind, and coconut. Cool.

DATE STICKS

1 cup sifted flour   1 teaspoon Calumet Baking Powder
½ teaspoon salt   1 cup sugar   2 eggs, well beaten
1 tablespoon melted butter   2 cups dates, seeded and finely cut
½ cup nut meats, broken   1 tablespoon hot water

Sift flour once, measure, add baking powder and salt, and sift together three times. Add sugar gradually to eggs. Add butter. Beat in dates and nuts. Add flour, alternately with hot water, beating well after each addition. Divide mixture into two greased pans, 8x8x2 inches, and spread batter thin. Bake in slow oven (325° F.) 30 to 35 minutes. Cool. Cut in strips, 2⅔x1 inches. Remove from pans. Roll in powdered sugar. Makes 48.

✿

SUMMER DESSERT WAFFLES

2½ cups sifted Swans Down Cake Flour   2½ teaspoons Calumet Baking Powder
2 teaspoons sugar   2 egg yolks, well beaten   1½ cups milk
⅔ cup melted butter   2 egg whites, stiffly beaten

Sift flour once, measure, add baking powder and sugar, and sift again. Combine egg yolks, milk, and butter. Add to flour, beating until smooth. Fold in egg whites. Bake in hot waffle iron. Cool waffle. Serve in sections, topped with ice cream and fruit sauce. Makes five 4-section waffles.

✿

BROWNIES

¾ cup sifted Swans Down Cake Flour
½ teaspoon Calumet Baking Powder   ⅓ cup butter or other shortening
2 squares Baker's Unsweetened Chocolate, melted   1 cup sugar
2 eggs, well beaten   1 teaspoon vanilla
½ cup walnut meats, chopped

Sift flour once, measure, add baking powder, and sift again. Add butter to chocolate and blend. Combine sugar and eggs; add chocolate mixture, beating thoroughly, then flour, vanilla, and nuts. Bake in greased pan, 8x8x2 inches, in moderate oven (350° F.) 35 minutes. Cut into squares.

✿

OLD-FASHIONED NUT LOAF
(3 eggs)

2 cups sifted Swans Down Cake Flour   2 teaspoons Calumet Baking Powder
½ teaspoon salt   ⅔ cup butter or other shortening   1 cup sugar
3 eggs, unbeaten   1 cup nut meats, finely cut
6 tablespoons milk   1 teaspoon vanilla

Sift flour once, measure, add baking powder and salt, and sift together three times. Cream butter thoroughly, add sugar gradually, and cream together until light and fluffy. Add eggs, one at a time, beating thoroughly after each addition. Add nuts and blend. Add flour, alternately with milk, a small amount at a time. Beat after each addition until smooth. Add vanilla. Bake in greased loaf pan in moderate oven (350° F.) 1¼ hours.

Whether it is a bril- liant May morning or an August day that threat- ens to be too hot and too long, a porch breakfast casts a magic spell. Choose a sunny corner, lay the table with a gay, crisp cloth; add a bowl of fresh-picked flowers. Then watch a simple meal turn into a festival and the weariest mortals become benevolent gods.

MENU SUGGESTION 5

POST TOASTIES WITH BERRIES	CUBED ORANGES
SCRAMBLED EGGS BACON	*WHOLE BRAN GRIDDLE CAKES
*CURRANT COFFEE ROLLS	BREAKFAST SAUSAGES
COFFEE	COFFEE
☼	☼
SLICED PEACHES GRAPE-NUTS	HOT CEREAL WITH CREAM
SAUTÉED TOMATOES	GRILLED HAM AND PINEAPPLE
FRIZZLED BEEF	ORANGE MARMALADE
*CREAM DROP BISCUITS	*GRAHAM MUFFINS
COFFEE	COFFEE

A tempting hot bread rescues any breakfast from the common- place. Particularly when it is chosen with an eye to the season, and is accompanied by a good cup of Maxwell House Coffee.

Recipes for dishes marked [*] are on pages 88 and 122.

Breakfast in key with the season

*The proper table arrange-
ment for a dessert served
by the hostess*

An army of butlers
would not serve a dessert
with greater dignity and
beauty than can the
hostess who sits at this
table. The dessert plates,
arranged in two piles, are
placed directly in front
of the hostess; above
them, the dessert, with a
serving knife and spoon.
Only the silver and china
needed for this course
are left upon the table.

MENU SUGGESTION 6

*RASPBERRY BLITZ TORTE	*FRUITED SPONGE TORTE
PASTEL SUGAR CANDIES	SALTED NUTS
COFFEE	TEA
☼	☼
*HUNGARIAN CHOCOLATE CAKE	*BANANA NUT CAKE
FRESH SUMMER PEARS	RAISIN CLUSTERS
ICED COFFEE	COFFEE

Blitz Torte with fresh berries—unusual, delicious, and colorful—
is a dessert to serve at the table. Banana Nut Cake, Hungarian Chocolate Cake, and Fruited Sponge Torte also claim your attention.

Recipes for dishes marked [*] are on pages 74 and 123.

A gala dessert served at the table

WHOLE BRAN GRIDDLE CAKES

1¾ cups milk   1 cup Post's Whole Bran   1½ cups sifted flour
3 teaspoons Calumet Baking Powder   2 teaspoons sugar   1 teaspoon salt
2 eggs, well beaten   1 tablespoon melted butter

Pour milk over Post's Whole Bran. Sift flour once, measure, add baking powder, sugar, and salt, and sift again. Add eggs to bran mixture. Add flour and blend. Add butter. Bake on hot, well-greased griddle. Serve hot with butter and Log Cabin Syrup. Makes 2 dozen griddle cakes.

✺

CREAM DROP BISCUITS

2 cups sifted Swans Down Cake Flour   2 teaspoons Calumet Baking Powder
1 tablespoon sugar   ½ teaspoon salt   ⅔ cup heavy cream   ¼ cup milk

Sift flour once, measure, add baking powder, sugar, and salt, and sift again. Combine cream and milk; add to flour mixture all at once and stir carefully until all flour is dampened. Then stir vigorously until mixture forms a soft dough that clings to sides of bowl. Drop from teaspoon on ungreased baking sheet. Bake in hot oven (450° F.) 12 to 15 minutes. Makes 18.

✺

GRAHAM MUFFINS OR GEMS

1 cup sifted flour   1 teaspoon salt   3 teaspoons Calumet Baking Powder
4 tablespoons sugar   1¾ cups Graham flour   1 egg, well beaten
1½ cups milk   1 tablespoon melted butter or other shortening

Sift flour once, measure, add salt, baking powder, and sugar, and sift again. Add Graham flour. Combine egg, milk, and shortening. Add to flour, beating only enough to dampen all flour. Bake in greased muffin or gem pans in hot oven (425° F.) 25 minutes. Makes 18 muffins or gems.

✺

NUT CRUMB COFFEE CAKE

2 cups sifted Swans Down Cake Flour   2 teaspoons Calumet Baking Powder
½ teaspoon salt   3 tablespoons butter or other shortening
1 cup sugar   1 cup milk   ½ teaspoon vanilla
2 tablespoons sugar   ¾ teaspoon cinnamon   ¾ cup soft bread crumbs
2 tablespoons melted butter   2 tablespoons walnut meats, finely chopped

Sift flour once, measure, add baking powder and salt, and sift again. Cream butter, add sugar gradually, and cream together well. Add flour, alternately with milk, beating after each addition until smooth. Add vanilla. Turn into greased pan, 9x9x2 inches. Combine sugar and cinnamon, mix with crumbs, add melted butter and nuts, and sprinkle over cake. Bake in moderate oven (350° F.) 45 minutes. Cut in squares in pan and remove each square carefully so that the nut-crumb topping will not crumble. Serve hot with coffee.

This coffee cake is rich, sweet, and tender. It is suitable for breakfast and delicious served as a tea cake or luncheon dessert.

RASPBERRY BLITZ TORTE
(4 eggs)

1⅓ cups sifted Swans Down Cake Flour	1⅓ teaspoons Calumet Baking Powder

½ cup butter or other shortening

½ cup sugar   4 egg yolks, unbeaten   5 tablespoons milk

4 egg whites   1 cup sugar   1 quart raspberries, sweetened

Sift flour once, measure, add baking powder, and sift together three times. Cream butter thoroughly, add sugar gradually, and cream together until light and fluffy. Add egg yolks, one at a time, beating very thoroughly after each addition. Add flour, alternately with milk, a small amount at a time, beating well. Spread in two greased 9-inch layer pans.

Beat egg whites until foamy throughout. Add sugar, 2 tablespoons at a time; beat after each addition until sugar is thoroughly blended. After all sugar is added, continue beating until mixture will stand in peaks. Spread in equal amounts on top of each layer. Bake in slow oven (325° F.) 25 minutes, then increase heat to moderate (350° F.) and bake 30 minutes longer. Spread sweetened raspberries between layers and top with whipped cream and raspberries. Cut in wedges for serving.

✿

BANANA NUT CAKE
(2 eggs)

2¼ cups sifted Swans Down Cake Flour   2¼ teaspoons Calumet Baking Powder

¼ teaspoon salt   ½ cup butter or other shortening

1 cup sugar   2 eggs, well beaten   ¾ cup milk   1 teaspoon vanilla

Sift flour once, measure, add baking powder and salt, and sift together three times. Cream butter thoroughly, add sugar gradually, and cream together until light and fluffy. Add eggs and beat well. Add flour, alternately with milk, a small amount at a time. Beat after each addition until smooth. Add vanilla. Bake in two greased 9-inch layer pans in moderate oven (375° F.) 25 minutes. When cool, cover bottom layer with sliced bananas. Over this pour Harvest Moon Frosting (page 106). Place second layer on top and cover top and sides of cake with remaining frosting.

✿

HUNGARIAN CHOCOLATE CREAM CAKE
(2 eggs)

2 cups sifted Swans Down Cake Flour   2 teaspoons Calumet Baking Powder

½ teaspoon salt   1 cup sugar   2 eggs, well beaten

1¼ cups heavy cream   1 teaspoon vanilla

Sift flour once, measure, add baking powder and salt, and sift together three times. Add sugar gradually to eggs, and beat well. Add flour, alternately with cream, a small amount at a time. Beat after each addition until smooth. Add vanilla. Bake in a greased pan, 8x8x2 inches, in moderate oven (350° F.) 50 minutes. Spread Hungarian Chocolate Frosting and Filling (page 108) on top and sides of cake. (May also be baked in greased, fluted round pan and served unfrosted.)

*If you are hostess and cook,
entertain your friends
with buffet suppers*

Buffet suppers, popula[r]
affairs that they alway[s]
are, solve many a prob[-]
lem for the hostess wh[o]
has many friends an[d]
few, if any, servants. Th[e]
menu should be s[o]
planned that it may a[ll]
be placed on the tabl[e]
at once; the linen, sil[-]
ver, dishes, and food s[o]
grouped that the gue[sts]
may make an order[ly]
journey around the tabl[e]

MENU SUGGESTION 7

CRAB MEAT EN CASSEROLE

*CREAM SCONES OR *CINNAMON DROP BISCUITS

SPICED RED CHERRIES

*REGAL CARAMEL CAKE OR *ORANGE CAKE

LEMON ICE

SALTED NUTS

COFFEE

Cream Scones, Crab Meat en Casserole, and Spiced Red Cherries
make an interesting and satisfying main course; yet one which
leaves just enough appetite for the full enjoyment of the dessert.

Recipes for dishes marked [*] are on pages 82 and 126.

A smart serve-yourself supper

*A charming form of hos-
pitality that anyone can
offer and all like

A carefully and attrac-
ively arranged tea table
oes a long way toward
nsuring the success of a
ea party, whether it's
or three or for thirty
riends. The tea service
nust be complete, dainty,
mmaculate. Remember
hat confusion and dis-
rder are enemies to the
ood conversation and
epose for which the tea
our stands, first of all.

MENU SUGGESTION 8

*THIN SLICES OF GENOESE CAKE
*LITTLE SPICE COOKIES
TEA
☼
*THIN NUT BREAD SANDWICHES
*LEMON BISCUITS
*COCONUT TEA STRIPS   *BROWNIES
CANDIED GRAPEFRUIT PEEL
TEA

Trim slices of Genoese Cake and Little Spice Cookies were chosen
for the tea illustrated. A more elaborate tea might prefer Nut Bread
Sandwiches, Lemon Biscuits, Coconut Tea Strips, and Brownies.

Recipes for dishes marked [*] are on pages 89, 115, 119, and 127.

Over the friendly cup of tea

CREAM SCONES

2 cups sifted Swans Down Cake Flour
2 teaspoons Calumet Baking Powder   ½ teaspoon salt
2 teaspoons sugar   4 tablespoons butter or other shortening
1 egg and 1 egg yolk, well beaten
⅓ cup light cream   1 egg white, slightly beaten   Sugar

Sift flour once, measure, add baking powder, salt, and sugar, and sift again.
Cut in shortening; add egg and cream all at once and stir carefully until
all flour is dampened. Then stir vigorously until mixture forms a soft
dough and follows spoon around bowl. Turn out immediately on slightly
floured board and knead 30 seconds. Roll ½ inch thick and cut in triangles.
Place on ungreased baking sheet. Brush tops lightly with egg white, and
sprinkle with sugar. Bake in hot oven (450° F.) 12 to 15 minutes. Makes 12.

☼

REGAL CARAMEL CAKE
(3 eggs)

2 cups sifted Swans Down Cake Flour
2 teaspoons Calumet Baking Powder   ½ teaspoon salt
⅔ cup butter or other shortening
1 cup sugar   3 eggs, well beaten   6 tablespoons milk
½ teaspoon vanilla   ¼ teaspoon lemon extract

Sift flour once, measure, add baking powder and salt, and sift together
three times. Cream butter thoroughly, add sugar gradually, and cream
together until light and fluffy. Add eggs and beat well. Add flour, alternately with milk, a small amount at a time. Beat after each addition until
smooth. Add flavoring. Bake in two greased 9-inch layer pans in moderate
oven (375° F.) 25 minutes, or until done. Spread Caramel Frosting (page
109) between layers and on top and sides of cake. Double recipe to make
three 10-inch layers. Sprinkle chopped nuts on sides of cake, if desired.

☼

ORANGE CAKE
(3 eggs)

2½ cups sifted Swans Down Cake Flour   2 teaspoons Calumet Baking Powder
¼ teaspoon salt   Grated rind of 1 lemon   Grated rind of 1 orange
⅔ cup butter or other shortening   1½ cups sugar   3 eggs, unbeaten
2 tablespoons lemon juice   5 tablespoons orange juice
2 tablespoons water

Sift flour once, measure, add baking powder and salt, and sift together
three times. Add lemon and orange rinds to butter, and cream thoroughly,
add sugar gradually, and cream together until light and fluffy. Add eggs
one at a time, beating thoroughly after each addition. Add flour, alternately with combined fruit juice and water, a small amount at a time.
Beat after each addition until smooth. Bake in two greased 9-inch layer
pans in moderate oven (375° F.) 20 minutes, or until done. Spread Orange
Butter Frosting (page 107) between layers and on top and sides of cake.

126

GENOESE CAKE

(4 eggs)

1½ cups sifted Swans Down Cake Flour
1½ teaspoons Calumet Baking Powder   ½ cup butter
1 cup powdered sugar   ½ teaspoon lemon extract   4 eggs, well beaten

Sift flour once, measure, add baking powder, and sift together three times. Cream butter thoroughly, add sugar gradually, and cream together until light and fluffy. Add flavoring. Add eggs, alternately with flour, a small amount at a time, beating thoroughly after each addition. Turn into a greased pan, 8x8x2 inches, lined with greased paper. Bake in moderate oven (350° F.) 50 minutes.

Genoese Cake is of the pound cake type. Its even texture and delicate richness make it especially suitable to serve unfrosted. It should be cut in thin, dainty slices and served for tea or as an accompaniment for fruit desserts, or ice cream, sherbet, or water ice.

✿

LITTLE SPICE COOKIES

3¼ cups sifted Swans Down Cake Flour
3¼ teaspoons Calumet Baking Powder
½ teaspoon salt   ½ cup sugar   1 teaspoon cinnamon
¾ teaspoon ginger   ¾ teaspoon cloves   ½ teaspoon soda   1 egg, well beaten
⅓ cup melted butter or other shortening   1 cup molasses

Sift flour once, measure, add baking powder, salt, sugar, spices, and soda, and sift together three times. Combine egg, butter, and molasses in bowl. Add flour mixture and blend. Chill until firm enough to shape. Shape into small balls about ¾ inch in diameter. Roll in sugar or tiny colored candies. Bake on greased baking sheet in moderate oven (375° F.) 10 minutes, or until done. Makes 5 dozen little spice cookies.

✿

COCONUT TEA STRIPS

2 cups sifted Swans Down Cake Flour
2 teaspoons Calumet Baking Powder   1 tablespoon grated orange rind
4 tablespoons butter or other shortening
1 cup sugar   1 egg, unbeaten   ¼ cup milk   ½ cup orange juice
4 tablespoons sugar   1 egg white, stiffly beaten
½ can Baker's Coconut, Southern Style

Sift flour once, measure, add baking powder, and sift together three times. Add orange rind to butter and cream thoroughly. Add sugar gradually and cream together well. Add egg and beat until light and fluffy. Add flour, alternately with milk and orange juice, a small amount at a time. Beat after each addition until smooth. Pour into a greased pan, 15x10 inches. Cover with thin layer of meringue made by beating sugar into egg white. Sprinkle with coconut. Bake in moderate oven (350° F.) 25 minutes. Cool. Cut into strips. Makes 2 dozen tea strips. These tea cakes are also attractive when cut in diamond-shaped pieces.

In such a charming setting the simplest of food seems festive

A delightful, gracio͏us custom, and one whic͏h will give individuality ͏to informal entertaining, ͏is the serving of dessert ͏or of evening refreshmen͏ts around the hearth. Cak͏es which may be serve͏d in a very simple wa͏y and a beverage, make ͏a good fireside dessert. A͏r range the cake and be͏v erage service attractive͏ly on a coffee table or tra͏y

---

MENU SUGGESTION 9

*DIXIE WHITE CAKE OR *SUNSHINE CAKE
HOT CHOCOLATE

☼

*PRUNE CAKE OR *CHERRY PIE
SALTED NUTS   COFFEE

☼

*DOUGHNUTS OR *OLD-FASHIONED SUGAR COOKIES
SPICED PEACHES
COFFEE OR CIDER

Dixie White Cake, Prune Cake, and Doughnuts are star performers in fireside menus. They are easy to eat, distinct in character, and very good. With an appropriate beverage, they always win applause.

Recipes for dishes marked [*] are on pages 60, 69, 98, and 130.

Informally served by the fireside

Small table, small chairs, little cakes and hares, ready for a party!

The best of children's parties is the one that turns the "refreshments" into one of the child's regular meals. At the end of the party, after the frolicking and fun, give all of the small guests a simple supper or luncheon and send them home to bed or for a nap on schedule. Then everyone will be happy—even the bothersome grown-ups.

MENU SUGGESTION 10

CREAMED CHICKEN ON GRAHAM TOAST
CURRANT JELLY   CRISP CELERY
*BIRTHDAY CANDLE CAKES   COCOA

☼

CREAM OF CORN SOUP
WITH POP CORN GARNISH
MOLDED FRUIT SALAD WITH COOKED DRESSING
*HONEY BISCUITS
*PATTY'S BIRTHDAY CAKE   COCOA

Any good child who eats all the main course of his supper, and drinks his cocoa, deserves a Candle Cake, or a piece of Patty's Birthday Cake, looking as though it came straight from Fairyland.

Recipes for dishes marked [*] are on page 131.

A party for a little girl or boy

129

DIXIE WHITE CAKE

(Coconut baked in mixture)

(4 egg whites)

3 cups sifted Swans Down Cake Flour   3 teaspoons Calumet Baking Powder
1 teaspoon salt   ½ cup butter or other shortening   1½ cups sugar
1 cup water   1 teaspoon lemon extract
1 cup Baker's Coconut, Premium Shred   4 egg whites, stiffly beaten

Sift flour once, measure, add baking powder and salt, and sift together three times. Cream butter thoroughly, add sugar gradually, and cream together until light and fluffy. Add flour, alternately with water, a small amount at a time. Beat after each addition until smooth. Add lemon extract and coconut. Beat until well mixed. Fold in egg whites gently, but thoroughly. Bake in a greased pan, 8x8x2 inches, in moderate oven (350° F.) 1 hour and 15 minutes, or until done. Spread Orange Butter Frosting (page 107) on top and sides of cake. May also be served unfrosted.

Because of the coconut in the mixture Dixie White Cake will stay moist and delicious for several days after baking. The flavor is improved or mellowed by storing for a short time.

☼

PRUNE CAKE

(2 eggs)

2½ cups sifted Swans Down Cake Flour   ¾ teaspoon Calumet Baking Powder
1 teaspoon soda   1 teaspoon cloves   1 teaspoon allspice
1 teaspoon cinnamon   ½ cup butter or other shortening
1½ cups sugar   2 eggs, well beaten
1 cup cooked prunes, seeded and coarsely cut   1 cup sour milk or buttermilk

Sift flour once, measure, add baking powder, soda, and spices, and sift together three times. Cream butter thoroughly, add sugar gradually, and cream together until light and fluffy. Add eggs and prunes. Then add flour, alternately with milk, a small amount at a time, beating well after each addition. Bake in two greased 9-inch layer pans in moderate oven (375° F.) 25 to 30 minutes. Spread Caramel Frosting (page 109) between layers and on top and sides of cake. May also be served unfrosted.

☼

DOUGHNUTS

4 cups sifted flour   4 teaspoons Calumet Baking Powder   ½ teaspoon salt
¼ teaspoon nutmeg   1 cup sugar   2 eggs, well beaten
2 tablespoons melted butter or other shortening   1 cup milk
¼ teaspoon lemon extract

Sift flour once, measure, add baking powder, salt, and nutmeg, and sift together three times. Combine sugar and eggs; add shortening. Add flour, alternately with milk, a small amount at a time. Beat after each addition until smooth. Add flavoring. Knead lightly on slightly floured board. Roll ⅓ inch thick. Cut with floured doughnut cutter. Fry in deep fat (385° F.) until golden brown, turning frequently. Drain on unglazed paper. Sugar if desired. Makes 4 dozen small doughnuts.

BIRTHDAY CANDLE CAKES

(2 eggs)

1⅔ cups sifted Swans Down Cake Flour
1½ teaspoons Calumet Baking Powder
⅓ cup butter or other shortening   1 cup sugar   2 eggs, well beaten
½ cup milk   1 teaspoon lemon or vanilla extract

Sift flour once, measure, add baking powder, and sift together three times. Cream butter thoroughly, add sugar gradually, and cream together until light and fluffy. Add eggs, then flour, alternately with milk, a small amount at a time. Beat after each addition until smooth. Add flavoring. Pour into greased cup-cake pans, filling them about ⅔ full. Bake in moderate oven (375° F.) 20 minutes, or until done. Cool. Cover each cake with Seven Minute Frosting (page 104) and sprinkle thickly with Baker's Coconut, Southern Style. Arrange on large platter and insert candle holder with tiny candle in each cake. Light candles just before serving. Makes 24.

✿

HONEY BISCUITS

2 cups sifted flour
2 teaspoons Calumet Baking Powder   ½ teaspoon salt
4 tablespoons butter or other shortening   ¾ cup milk (about)

4 tablespoons butter   ½ cup honey

Sift flour once, measure, add baking powder and salt, and sift again. Cut in shortening. Add milk gradually, stirring until soft dough is formed. Turn out on slightly floured board and knead 30 seconds, or enough to shape. Roll ½ inch thick and cut with 2-inch floured biscuit cutter. Bake on ungreased baking sheet in hot oven (450° F.) 12 to 15 minutes. Remove biscuits from oven; split in halves. Spread lower halves with butter, and upper halves with honey. Put halves together and let stand a few minutes so that flavor may permeate biscuits. Makes 12.

✿

PATTY'S BIRTHDAY CAKE

(2 egg whites)

2 cups sifted Swans Down Cake Flour
2 teaspoons Calumet Baking Powder   ¼ teaspoon salt
4 tablespoons butter or other shortening
1 cup sugar   2 egg whites, unbeaten   ¾ cup milk
¼ teaspoon vanilla   ¼ teaspoon almond extract

Sift flour once, measure, add baking powder and salt, and sift together three times. Cream butter thoroughly, add sugar gradually, and cream together well. Add egg whites, one at a time, beating very thoroughly after each addition. Add flour, alternately with milk, a small amount at a time. Beat after each addition until smooth. Add flavoring. Bake in a greased pan, 8x8x2 inches, in moderate oven (350° F.) 50 minutes. Cover cake with Seven Minute Frosting (page 104) and sprinkle with Baker's Coconut, Southern Style, tinted. Insert candle holders with candles.

131

Picnics can be the best or the worst of meals, and successful ones do not just happen. Into them go carefully selected foods which will keep their freshness after a journey. Here we see two excellent picnic cakes. Maraschino Cherry Cake has a topping instead of a frosting, and Plantation Marble Cake needs neither.

MENU SUGGESTION 11

BAKED VIRGINIA HAM   POTATO CHIPS
*PETER PAN EARS OF CORN   TOMATOES
MUSTARD PICKLES   BEVERAGE
*PLANTATION MARBLE CAKE   FRESH FRUIT

☼

POTATO, CUCUMBER, AND RADISH SALAD
MEAT LOAF SANDWICHES   DILL PICKLES
DEVILED EGGS   BEVERAGE
*MARASCHINO CHERRY CAKE   PLUMS

Peter Pan Ears of Corn make a welcome change from sandwiches. They are especially good with baked ham and tomatoes. Top off the picnic with Plantation Marble Cake or Maraschino Cherry Cake.

Recipes for dishes marked [*] are on page 134.

Practical treats for picnics

*It is such fun to make them,
exciting to wrap them,
and oh! to eat them*

Its attractive shape, its garnish of holly and hard-sauce rosettes, its moist, rich goodness — all help this Christmas Plum Pudding to play a main rôle in the Christmas dinner. One of the Calumet Fruit Cakes, in gay wrappings, goes to a friend. The Holiday Fruit Cake in the foreground, so beautifully sliced, is ready for a holiday tea.

MENU SUGGESTION 12

GRAPEFRUIT AND TOKAY COCKTAIL
ROAST TURKEY WITH CELERY STUFFING
GIBLET GRAVY
MASHED POTATOES   CREAMED ONIONS
BAKED SQUASH   CRANBERRY SAUCE
ENDIVE SALAD WITH CHIFFONADE DRESSING
*CHRISTMAS PLUM PUDDING OR *FRUIT CAKE
CANDIES   NUTS
DEMI-TASSE

It is best to make these holiday desserts two or three weeks before Christmas, so that they will have time to ripen. Store them in air-tight containers, and put them away in a cool, dry place.

Recipes for dishes marked [*] are on page 135.

Christmas cakes and puddings

PETER PAN EARS OF CORN

1 cup yellow corn meal   1 teaspoon salt
2 tablespoons sugar   1 cup boiling water   ½ cup sifted flour
2½ teaspoons Calumet Baking Powder   ⅓ cup milk
1 egg, well beaten   ¼ cup melted butter or other shortening

Combine corn meal, salt, and sugar. Stir in boiling water and set aside to cool slightly. Sift flour once, measure, add baking powder, and sift again. Add milk, egg, and shortening to hot meal, then add flour, beating only enough to dampen all flour. Bake in greased corn-ear or muffin pans in hot oven (425° F.) 20 to 25 minutes. Makes 12 ears of corn.

☼

PLANTATION MARBLE CAKE

(2 eggs)

2 cups sifted Swans Down Cake Flour
2 teaspoons Calumet Baking Powder   ¼ teaspoon salt
½ cup butter or other shortening   1 cup sugar
2 eggs, well beaten   ⅔ cup milk   1 teaspoon cinnamon
½ teaspoon cloves   ½ teaspoon nutmeg   2 tablespoons molasses

Sift flour once, measure, add baking powder and salt, and sift together three times. Cream butter thoroughly, add sugar gradually, and cream together until light and fluffy. Add eggs; then flour, alternately with milk, a small amount at a time. Beat after each addition until smooth. Divide batter into two parts. To one part, add spices and molasses. Put by tablespoons into greased loaf pan, 8x4x3 inches, alternating the light and dark mixtures. Bake in moderate oven (350° F.) 1 hour and 15 minutes, or until done. Cut in slices for serving.

If desired, bake this cake in greased pan, 8x8x2 inches, in moderate oven (350° F.) 50 minutes. Spread Butter Frosting (page 107) on top and sides of cake. Decorate with chopped pecan meats and raisin clusters.

☼

MARASCHINO CHERRY CAKE

(2 eggs)

2 cups sifted Swans Down Cake Flour
2 teaspoons Calumet Baking Powder   ¼ teaspoon salt
⅓ cup butter or other shortening   1 cup sugar
2 eggs, well beaten   ⅔ cup milk   ½ teaspoon vanilla

½ cup walnut meats, finely broken   16 maraschino cherries, cut in eighths

Sift flour once, measure, add baking powder and salt, and sift together three times. Cream butter thoroughly, add sugar gradually, and cream together until light and fluffy. Add eggs and beat well. Add flour, alternately with milk, a small amount at a time. Beat after each addition until smooth. Add flavoring. Pour into a greased pan, 8x8x2 inches. Sprinkle nuts and cherries over top. Bake in moderate oven (350° F.) 1 hour, or until done. The nuts and cherries will stay on top of cake, if they have been finely cut. They give a colorful, attractive topping to the cake.

CHRISTMAS PLUM PUDDING

½ cup apple, chopped   ½ cup suet, chopped   ½ cup molasses
2 eggs, well beaten   ½ cup milk   2 cups sifted flour   ¼ cup figs, chopped
½ cup raisins   ½ cup currants   ¼ cup citron, sliced
¼ cup candied cherries, quartered   1 tablespoon candied orange peel, chopped
¼ cup almonds, blanched and chopped   2 teaspoons Calumet Baking Powder
½ teaspoon salt   ½ teaspoon soda   ½ teaspoon cinnamon
¼ teaspoon allspice   ½ teaspoon nutmeg

Combine apple, suet, molasses, eggs, and milk. Sift flour once; measure. Mix ½ cup flour with fruit and nuts. Combine remaining flour, baking powder, salt, soda, and spices, and sift again. Add to molasses mixture. Add fruit. Turn into well-greased molds, filling them ⅔ full. Cover tightly. Steam 3 hours. Serve hot with hard sauce. Serves 12.

✿

CALUMET FRUIT CAKE
(10 eggs)

1 pound (4½ cups) sifted Swans Down Cake Flour
1 teaspoon Calumet Baking Powder   ½ teaspoon cloves   ½ teaspoon cinnamon
½ teaspoon mace   1 pound butter or other shortening
1 pound brown sugar   10 eggs, well beaten   ½ pound candied cherries
½ pound candied pineapple   1 pound dates, seeded and sliced   1 pound raisins
1 pound currants   ½ pound citron, thinly sliced
½ pound candied orange and lemon peel   ½ pound nut meats, chopped
1 cup honey   1 cup molasses   ½ cup cider

Sift flour once, measure, add baking powder and spices, and sift together three times. Cream shortening thoroughly, add sugar gradually, and cream together until light and fluffy. Add remaining ingredients. Add flour gradually. Bake in four greased pans, 8x8x2 inches, lined with greased paper, in slow oven (250° F.) 3 to 3½ hours. Makes 10 pounds fruit cake.

✿

HOLIDAY CAKE
(5 egg whites)

1¾ cups sifted Swans Down Cake Flour
1 teaspoon Calumet Baking Powder   ¼ teaspoon salt
½ cup butter or other shortening   ¾ cup sugar
5 egg whites, unbeaten   ¼ cup candied cherries, finely cut
½ cup citron, finely cut   ½ cup seedless raisins
½ cup almonds, chopped   ¾ cup Baker's Coconut, Premium Shred
½ teaspoon almond extract   ½ teaspoon vanilla

Sift flour once, measure, add baking powder and salt, and sift together three times. Cream butter thoroughly, add sugar gradually, and cream together until light and fluffy. Add egg whites, one at a time, beating after each addition until thoroughly blended. Add fruit, nuts, coconut, and flavoring, and mix well. Add flour, a small amount at a time. Beat after each addition until smooth. Bake in a greased loaf pan, 8x4x3 inches, lined with greased paper, in slow oven (300° F.) 1 hour and 15 minutes.

Take that hurry-worry out of your baking— here's the way!

Guests coming for th
week-end always mea
to the hostess, "Wh
shall I have for dessert?
But here is a bright ne
answer. Mix this recip
for Miracle Cake—
makes three temptin
cake-desserts. Divid
batter into pans, wra
store in refrigerator, an
bake as needed. For th
convenience, praise be t
Calumet's Double Actio

MENU SUGGESTION 13

First Day
*PRUNE-APRICOT UPSIDE DOWN CAKE

Second Day	*Third Day*
*SPICED PECAN CAKES	*WASHINGTON PIE

☼

First Day
*PECAN TORTE OR *FAVORITE JAM SQUARES

Second Day	*Third Day*
*COTTAGE PUDDING	*CURRANT CUP CAKES

Here are suggestions for two different series of week-end desserts, each group made by one mixing of Miracle Cake batter. The menus on the opposite page use the desserts from the first group.

Recipes for dishes marked [*] are on pages 138 and 139.

From this one easy mixing job

ree delicious cake desserts
—one for each day
of the week-end

rune-apricot Upside
own Cake is the treat
r the first day's din-
r. Next day's luncheon
ings fresh, warm
iced Pecan Cakes.
en, as a triumphant
max, comes Washing-
n Pie, as airy-light, as
lvety of crumb, as any
ke mixed and baked
mediately. Complete
enus below, and direc-
ns for cakes on page 138.

ns for cakes on page 138.

MENU SUGGESTION 13 (*cont.*)

First Day—Dinner
JELLIED TOMATO BOUILLON
BAKED HALIBUT   POTATOES CHANTILLY   SWISS CHARD
*PRUNE-APRICOT UPSIDE DOWN CAKE   COFFEE

✿

Second Day—Luncheon
LETTUCE AND BACON SANDWICHES
MILK   *SPICED PECAN CAKES   FRUIT

✿

Third Day—Supper
CHEESE SOUFFLÉ   BUTTERED ROLLS   OLIVE RELISH
*WASHINGTON PIE   ICED POSTUM

Recipes for dishes marked [*] are on page 138.

Three glorious week-end desserts

MIRACLE CAKE

4⅔ cups sifted Swans Down Cake Flour
4½ teaspoons Calumet Baking Powder   ½ teaspoon salt
1 cup butter or other shortening   2 cups sugar   4 eggs, well beaten
1½ cups milk   2 teaspoons vanilla

Sift flour once, measure, add baking powder and salt, and sift together
three times. Cream butter thoroughly, add sugar gradually, and cream
together until light and fluffy. Add eggs and mix well. Add flour, alternately with milk, a small amount at a time. Beat after each addition until
smooth. Add vanilla. Divide batter into pans for storing and baking in any
three of the ways suggested on these two pages.

✿

PRUNE-APRICOT UPSIDE DOWN CAKE

4 tablespoons butter   ½ cup brown sugar, firmly packed
13 cooked apricots   6 cooked prunes, halved and seeded
Miracle Cake batter (above)

Melt butter in an 8x8x2-inch pan over low flame. Add sugar; stir until
melted. On this arrange apricots and prunes, cut-side up, alternating an
apricot with a prune half. Pour about ⅓ of Miracle Cake batter over contents of pan. Bake at once in moderate oven (350° F.) 50 minutes, or until
done. Loosen cake from sides and bottom of pan with spatula. Serve upside down on dish with fruit on top. Garnish with whipped cream. This
upside down cake may be served hot or cold.

✿

SPICED PECAN CAKES

2½ tablespoons molasses   ½ teaspoon cloves
½ teaspoon nutmeg   1 teaspoon cinnamon   Miracle Cake batter (above)

1 tablespoon melted butter   2 tablespoons brown sugar
¼ cup pecan meats, finely chopped

Add molasses and spices to about ⅓ of Miracle Cake batter and beat well.
Pour into 16 large- or 24 medium-sized greased cup-cake pans, filling them
⅔ full. Cover closely with damp cloth, then waxed paper, tie securely, and
store in refrigerator until cakes are to be baked. Bake in moderate oven
(375° F.) 20 minutes, or until done. Before removing from oven, combine
melted butter and sugar, add pecans, and mix; sprinkle mixture on top of
cakes and bake 2 or 3 minutes longer. These Spiced Pecan Cakes are excellent served with milk and fruit for a luncheon dessert.

✿

WASHINGTON PIE

Pour about ⅓ of the Miracle Cake batter (above) into two greased 8-inch
layer pans. Cover closely with damp cloth, then waxed paper, tie securely,
and store in refrigerator until cake is to be baked. Bake in moderate oven
(375° F.) 25 minutes, or until done. Cool. Spread raspberry jam between
layers. Sift powdered sugar over top of cake.

PECAN TORTE

Miracle Cake batter (page 138)   2 egg whites   ½ cup sugar
½ cup pecan meats, coarsely broken   ½ cup cream, whipped   Pecans

Pour about ⅓ of Miracle Cake batter into one 8-inch layer pan. Cover closely with damp cloth, then waxed paper, tie securely, and store in refrigerator until cake is to be baked. When cake is to be baked, beat egg whites until foamy throughout. Add sugar, 2 tablespoons at a time, beating after each addition until sugar is thoroughly blended. After all sugar is added, continue beating until mixture will stand in peaks. Spread meringue on top of batter. Sprinkle with nuts. Bake in slow oven (325° F.) 25 minutes, then increase heat to moderate (350° F.) and bake 30 minutes longer. To serve, spread with whipped cream and garnish with pecans.

☼

COTTAGE PUDDING

2½ tablespoons molasses   ½ teaspoon cloves   Miracle Cake batter (page 138)
½ teaspoon nutmeg   1 teaspoon cinnamon

Add molasses and spices to about ⅓ of Miracle Cake batter and beat well. Turn at once into a greased pan, 8x8x2 inches. Cover closely with damp cloth, then waxed paper, tie securely, and store in refrigerator until pudding is to be baked. Bake in moderate oven (350° F.) 45 minutes. Serve hot with Crimson Rhubarb Sauce.

Crimson Rhubarb Sauce

2 cups rhubarb, washed and cut in ½-inch pieces   ½ cup water
2 cups strawberries, washed, hulled, and cut in half   1 cup sugar

Combine all ingredients and cook until fruit is tender. Makes about 3½ cups sauce. Use red-stalked rhubarb, if possible.

☼

FAVORITE JAM SQUARES

Pour about ⅓ of Miracle Cake batter (page 138) into greased pan, 8x8x2 inches, cover closely with damp cloth, then waxed paper, tie securely, and store in refrigerator until cake is to be baked. Bake in moderate oven (350° F.) 50 minutes, or until done. Cool. Top with ½ cup of any favorite jam folded into ½ cup cream, whipped. Cut in squares for serving.

Miracle Cake batter may also be baked in large greased cup-cake pans. When cool the center of each cake may be partly removed, and the cakes filled with any favorite jam and topped with whipped cream.

☼

CURRANT CUP CAKES

Pour about ⅓ of Miracle Cake batter (page 138) into 16 large- or 24 medium-sized greased cup-cake pans, filling them ⅔ full. Sprinkle currants or seedless raisins over tops of cakes. Cover closely with damp cloth, then waxed paper, tie securely, and store in refrigerator until cakes are to be baked. Bake in moderate oven (375° F.) 20 minutes, or until done.

General Index
All About Home Baking

Note: Black numbers indicate recipe pages

Note: Black numbers indicate recipe pages

Note: Black numbers indicate recipe pages

Note: Black numbers indicate recipe pages

Note: Black numbers indicate recipe pages

PHOTOGRAPHS BY H. I. WILLIAMS · · · COMPOSITION BY
NEW YORK MONOTYPE COMPOSITION CO. · · · ENGRAVINGS
BY GALVANOTYPE ENGRAVING CO. · · · PRINTING BY CONDÉ
NAST PRESS · · · BINDING BY J. F. TAPLEY CO. · · · NEW YORK